PARENT ALERT!
HOW TO
KEEP YOUR
KIDS SAFE
ONLINE

PARENT ALERT!

HOW TO KEEP YOUR KIDS SAFE ONLINE

SECURITY EXPERT
WILL GEDDES

WITH
NADIA SAWALHA & KAYE ADAMS

CONTENTS

WILL'S PERSPECTIVE

The online world is evolving and expanding so rapidly on a daily basis that it's highly likely some major developments have probably occurred even since I finished writing this. Which is why we need to adjust and adapt continually to this ever-changing digital and virtual landscape. The Internet is complicated enough for us adults; it's even more so for our children.

Most of us probably manage our entire lives from one device: our family, friends, work, school, calls, messages, photos, videos, education, shopping, social media, entertainment, and finances. It's not a way of life—it IS our life.

As convenient as this may be, it has blurred the line between the adult and child worlds, placing pressure on children to act like adults at an earlier age. The average child receives their first phone at the age of 11, and children as young as 3 or 4 have access to their parents' tablets or laptops—tools that expose them to the largely unrestricted and unmoderated world of the Internet.

The saturation of social media images that children are exposed to can give them unrealistic expectations of the real world, setting impossible standards of beauty and lifestyle. It's not uncommon for children as young as 10 or 11 to encounter pornography, too; for some, it might even be their sole form of sexual education.

Children are also exposed online to cyberbullies, cyberstalkers, and trolls and might be encouraged to send sexts or watch horrifically violent or graphic content. This can influence their perception, expectations, and understanding of others and pollute their definition of what is and isn't acceptable behavior. It may be many, many years before we see the psychological impact this exposure ultimately has on future generations.

For more than 25 years, I've been working within the more specialist end of the security world, dealing with issues ranging from stalkers, cybercriminals, blackmail, and extortion to death threats and terrorism.

On my travels, I have met and worked alongside some of the very best hackers, coders, and programmers in the world and have had the privilege of learning an awful lot from them.

When friends and clients have approached me for advice on how to keep their children safe online, it's sometimes because they didn't know where else to go. The sheer quantity of information available online is overwhelming, and much of it can be of dubious trustworthiness, varying in its message, or even entirely contradictory. This can prove extremely frustrating for a panicking parent whose child has found themselves caught up in the darker parts of the web.

This book has been created as a means of filtering all that information into a format that, hopefully, even those with limited technological knowledge can understand. It's a practical and realistic take on the genuine risks children face. Some of my advice may be considered extreme, but we need to keep things in perspective: children are banned from drinking alone until age 18 in most countries, but parents in those same countries will give their children smartphones that allow unfiltered access to everything the Internet has to offer.

Have I covered everything? Possibly and probably not because, in reality, each chapter here could easily provide a whole book's worth of material all by itself. But I hope our book answers many of your questions and provides some guidance and solutions to steer your child through the Internet's dangerous, and often uncharted, waters.

Will Geddes

NADIA & KAYE'S PERSPECTIVE

What are they doing up there in their bedrooms on their phones? What are they looking at and listening to? Who are they talking to, and, more worryingly, who is talking to them? Are they being bullied? Are they being stalked? Are they being groomed? Would they be foolish enough to send compromising photos of themselves to some random person or say something that might haunt them for the rest of their lives? Will they turn out to be dysfunctional screen slaves, incapable of holding a normal conversation?

Nadia and I have these conversations all the time about our tweens and teens (four between us, aged between 10 and 15). We are not technophobes, and, to be absolutely honest, we could probably do with cutting down on our own screen time, but we've been around the block a few times—our daughters, however, are at a vulnerable age.

We've had the chats about sex and alcohol and drugs and all the dangers that might arise from them, but at least we vaguely know what we are talking about in those departments. When it comes to the online world, we feel hopelessly naive and are struggling to keep up.

It was back in early summer 2017 that a major alarm bell went off. It was not long after Snapchat, the site most beloved of our older girls, introduced a new feature called Snap Map, which gives users the capability to track their friends' whereabouts in real time.

We were blissfully ignorant of its existence until 14-year-old Maddie very patiently tried to explain it to Nadia. As the penny dropped, a bomb went off for us. Snap Map is a feature that allows young children to make themselves traceable at all times and in real time, showing not only their physical whereabouts and movements but also who they are with at any time.

The potential for mischief and misuse seemed to us to be immense, and, clearly, we were not alone.

We filmed a short Facebook video about Snap Map in which Nadia voiced her misgivings. It now has 28 MILLION hits! The video was shared hundreds of times and liked or commented on by more than 52,000 people.

To be fair, the response was polarized, with some people unconcerned about the level of exposure to risk Snap Maps gives, but there were many more who shared our concern.

It was then that we decided we'd like to spread the word among parents like ourselves about the potential dangers of online activity for our kids.

We know we are never going to put the genie back into the bottle, nor would we want to. This high-tech world, which will always be slightly foreign to us, is all our kids have ever known. It is their natural habitat, but it's still our job to help them navigate some of the more turbulent waters.

In reality, our little darlings might be able to whiz around a touch screen faster than we can count, but they don't always understand as much as they would have us believe, and their perception of potential danger tends to be casual, to say the least.

And that's where this book comes in. It's intended as a get-you-up-to-speed-quick manual for parents who want to be one step ahead—or at least on the same level—with their tech-savvy tweens and teens.

You can't protect them from risks if you don't know what those risks are.

To that end, we have partnered up with WONDERFUL WILL GEDDES! And, let us tell you, working with Will to put this book together has been one heck of an eye-opener for us—a seemingly innocent calculator app that is actually a portal for secret contacts and messages?! Who knew?!

Nadia Sawalha   **Kaye Adams**

TALKING TO YOUR KIDS

STARTING CONVERSATIONS AND BUILDING TRUST BETWEEN YOU AND YOUR KIDS

WHAT YOU NEED TO KNOW

KAYE'S EXPERIENCE

Nadia and I have very different parenting styles. Not that we fundamentally disagree, but we have different personalities, as do our partners and children. We also have different lifestyles; while Nadia's girls are homeschooled, my two go to conventional school. I am sure there are parenting gurus out there who offer blanket advice on how to deal with children, but, although we are always keen to hear from experts, we are unconvinced that one size fits all.

It tends to be a proud boast of many modern parents that their children "tell them everything," and until a couple of years ago, I would have wanted to believe that, too.

At time of writing, my daughters are 11 and 15, and the age gap has now become very significant. Although the little one will not necessarily volunteer everything right away, she'll usually want to get things off her chest at some point, especially if she is feeling upset or unhappy. In terms of keeping her in check, she's still of an age to respond to a heavy glare and a threat to hide the cookies.

My elder daughter, however, is a different story. It's not that she is deliberately disobedient—quite the contrary. She is hardworking, resourceful, and generally obliging, and I am immensely proud of her—but she is not a kid anymore. She is growing up and making her own judgments about the world and the people in it. While I would still like to think that she would come to me if she found herself in dire straits, I know that her friends are probably the major day-to-day influence in her life. Does she tell me everything? I very much doubt it.

Now, I am aware that this may sound like a sorry confession amounting to failure by modern-day parenting standards, but I wonder if we have set ourselves unrealistic goals these days. I enjoyed a wonderful relationship with both of my parents, for which I will always be grateful, but did I tell them everything? Did I hell! The practical reality is, I didn't need to.

In the absence of cell phones and digital technology, they often didn't have a clue where I was, who I was with, and what I was up to. They had no option but to trust that I would have the sense to keep myself safe. Would they have been there in a rush if I'd needed them? Yes! Were they breathing down my neck every minute of the day? No!

I might not have had a cell phone, data allowance, laptop, or tablet when I was a teenager, but I did have space to make mistakes and fix them myself. I passionately believe my children need that space, too, though I am not always able to hold the line.

For what it's worth, here's my advice: keep them close, but don't smother them. Don't go on and on about wishing smartphones and the Internet had never been invented—it will alienate them and fall on deaf ears. Find a neutral space to let the conversation flow naturally. For us, it is trudging through the park with the dog.

Lastly, make yourself fully aware of the potential dangers of the online world so you can keep ahead of the game. It's like when your child takes their first steps… you can scope out the sharp corners and uneven ground and be ready to catch them, but they need to learn to walk by themselves.

95%
of parents have **TALKED** to their teens about what **ONLINE CONTENT** is **APPROPRIATE** for them; **39%** do so **REGULARLY**.

NADIA'S EXPERIENCE

In my experience, the biggest mistake I can make with my girls if I'm wanting to have "a talk" about anything that they could deem "heavy" is to sit them down and eyeball them. I find that direct eye contact leaves our girls (and many of their peer group) feeling put on the spot and awkward. Such an approach invariably results in little more than a grunt and an irritable "I'm fine, Mom."

As a result, I try to do most of my serious communicating with them by stealth. And, believe it or not, the dreaded smartphone has become something of an ally when it comes to getting to the heart of the matter, certainly with our eldest.

Maddie is at that age when almost everything that she is going through feels like the end of the world. She also finds it hard (crikey, don't we all?!) to articulate how she's feeling about her innermost feelings, worries, and fears. What often happens when I think something is emotionally afoot is that I ask her if she's okay, to which she usually grunts, "Yeah," and, with her head firmly down, she shoots upstairs back to her room as fast as she possibly can.

In the early days, this caused me real anxiety and dread. But these days, I don't worry nearly so much, because Maddie and I have come to a useful agreement. We've agreed that whenever she feels shy or nervous about something, she can text me (under her own steam) to get the conversation started. Obviously, there are some things she never wants to share—as it should be and is for most teenagers—but 9 times out of 10, I will get a text at some point (maybe in the dead of night) reaching out to me and Mark, saying that she is in fact struggling with this or that.

Once the text is sent—hey, presto!—the dialogue is open! I make sure that I never overreact and stay as calm as I can. The last thing a struggling teen needs is someone shouting at them. Maddie now 100 percent trusts that my first priority is to establish that I love her and that I'm there for her.

My mantra is always, "A problem shared is a problem halved." Maddie often tells me that she advises her friends to open up to their parents, too, because ever since she has, she feels much better about everything. I couldn't bear the thought of going back to the old days before our agreement, when we were constantly in the dark as to what was going on. Some may think texting is a parent cop-out, but it really works for us, and, most importantly, it REALLY works for Maddie.

Maddie has also shared with us that the reason a lot of kids suffer in silence when things go wrong for them on social media is that they are terrified that their phone will be taken away from them. I have made a solemn promise that neither Mark nor I will ever take away her phone! This has definitely enabled a greater level of trust between us.

75% of **TEENS** say that having a **CELL PHONE** makes them feel **CLOSER** to their **PARENTS.**

I also think it's VERY important to show an interest in the things (especially on social media) that our children are "in to." I have to confess, my husband is much better at this than I am! So for instance, rather than just barking at them about what they are looking at, or how long they've been on their phones, I really ask them about what they are looking at, and I am often pleasantly surprised. Maddie was reading Shakespeare's sonnets one time— I thought she was texting a friend!

We also try to understand and appreciate those parts of social media or apps that are fun and engaging. As a family, we used to do lots of silly films on an app called Dubsmash. If your kids sense that you're not totally against the phone and their behavior around it, they tend to listen more when you do come down a little bit harder.

This tactic has taken an awful lot of heat out of "the phone thing," which, let's face it, is a highly addictive piece of tech that my husband and I introduced into their lives in the first place!

WILL'S EXPERT ANALYSIS

Trust is much more important than technology. You can install the toughest parental controls, follow the very best practices, and do every single thing I've recommended in this book, but there's still a chance that problems will arise.

It might not be anything as serious as a stranger trying to contact your child online. Children are naturally curious and adventurous, and I've seen plenty of examples where children saw parental control software as a challenge to be overcome. Sometimes children just want to see what it is you're trying to protect them from.

The best way to keep your child safe online is to communicate with them all the time, not just if you're worried about something. Casually ask them about the games they play, the apps they use, and who they talk to. As Nadia says, be interested in their online world: if you ask only occasionally, they'll think you're snooping.

Nadia and Kaye have also rightly pointed out that there's no right way to address these issues, and we all get it wrong sometimes. The best way to communicate can vary between children, and even

KAYE:
In a panic about the corrupting influence of social media, I installed some spyware on my teen daughter's phone with her knowledge. Our relationship went off a cliff, and the trust between us was totally destroyed. I became the last person she would confide in if anything went wrong. Our relationship recovered again as soon as the spyware was deleted.

the same child might want to communicate in different ways as they get older. Don't beat yourself up: all parents make mistakes, and we can learn from them and apply those lessons in the future.

In my view, the most common mistake is just saying "no" and not explaining why. That "why" is important, because it can often mean the difference between your child listening to you and your child tuning you out. You might want to tell a child simply not to visit a certain chat room; but if you also talk to them about the risk of getting horrible insults from complete strangers, it helps them to see why you don't want them on there. By giving them advice like: "Don't feed the trolls who are insulting you" (see p.71), you are also preparing them to deal with problems they encounter.

Talking, teaching, teamwork, and trust really matter. You might not realize that it's making a difference, but one day your child will come to you to ask for advice, your opinion, or your assistance. When they do, give yourself a pat on the back. You're #winning.

BROACHING THE SUBJECT

Try this method of starting a conversation about an online topic. It may help you build a sense of trust.

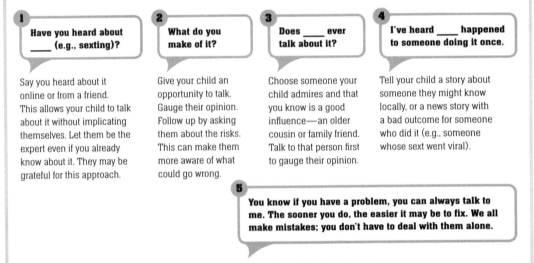

1 Have you heard about ____ (e.g., sexting)?

Say you heard about it online or from a friend. This allows your child to talk about it without implicating themselves. Let them be the expert even if you already know about it. They may be grateful for this approach.

2 What do you make of it?

Give your child an opportunity to talk. Gauge their opinion. Follow up by asking them about the risks. This can make them more aware of what could go wrong.

3 Does ____ ever talk about it?

Choose someone your child admires and that you know is a good influence—an older cousin or family friend. Talk to that person first to gauge their opinion.

4 I've heard ____ happened to someone doing it once.

Tell your child a story about someone they might know locally, or a news story with a bad outcome for someone who did it (e.g., someone whose sext went viral).

5 You know if you have a problem, you can always talk to me. The sooner you do, the easier it may be to fix. We all make mistakes; you don't have to deal with them alone.

WHAT ARE BEHAVIORAL WARNING SIGNS?

However frequently you communicate with your child about their online world, there may be times when they don't come to you about things—this is normal.

In most cases, the indicators that something has gone wrong are pretty similar between children and adults, although older children are often better at concealing things than younger ones. See the box (right) for a list of indicators that a child is experiencing a problem.

Each child is different, and their age will influence their reaction to a situation. Some of the signs on the list may apply and some may not. Be aware that your child might be deliberately concealing their emotions. I would recommend that you keep a note of any of these changes through a process I call "behavioral logging."

Behavioral logging

As a parent, you know your child better than anyone, so you are best placed to determine if there are any significant or noticeable changes in their normal behavior (although I know this can often be a challenge with teenagers).

This process might take some time; however, if there is a serious underlying issue, a new "pattern of behavior" will often quickly emerge. When you see any of the warning signs (see box, right) make a note of the **time and date**, your child's **behavior**, the physical **location**, and ideally which **site or app** they were using.

It is essential that you do this discreetly. If your child believes you are monitoring them (more than normal, that is) or spying on them, you could isolate them further and make the situation worse.

WHEN SHOULD I STEP IN?

Every child and situation is different, but I think these are pretty reliable red flags:

- **Your gut says something isn't right.** You know your child better than anyone, and if your instinct is telling you something is wrong, pay attention.
- **There's been a change in one or more warning signs**. If you see a marked deterioration in their behavior, you

WARNING SIGNS

These are all indications your child might be dealing with a problem:

- Irritability (more than usual)
- Loss of appetite
- Spontaneous emotional outbursts (shouting or crying)
- Inability to concentrate on even small tasks or duties
- Becoming withdrawn and/or avoiding family and friends
- Constantly needing attention or company
- Poor personal hygiene
- Concealing their device
- Visible anxiety when checking their device
- Insomnia
- Dramatic changes in presentation (e.g., wearing less flattering or more revealing clothes or heavy makeup)
- Excessive fidgeting, nail biting, or physical tics
- Regularly clearing their Internet history
- Anxiously checking their device or taking it somewhere private to read messages
- Installing new, innocuous apps on their device
- Online deliveries arriving unexpectedly
- Needing constant reassurance
- Self-harm

NADIA:
A friend told me that her boys chatter on about what's on their mind when they're in the back of the car. She thinks it's because they find it easier to open up when they can't see her face. So it might be worth trying to have these conversations while you are in the car. You could also try while kicking a ball around the yard or fixing a bike together.

need to intervene. This might happen over time, although serious changes might happen quickly enough that you feel you need to step in right away.

HOW DO I FIND OUT WHAT'S WRONG?

It's always best to take a nonaccusatory approach. If your child is in trouble, you're unlikely to get to the root of the problem by demanding explanations or apologies or by getting angry.

Consider whether your child would be more comfortable talking face to face, via instant message or text (as Nadia and her daughter do), or while doing something they enjoy. Maybe try them all. It'll be obvious pretty quickly which approach your child finds best for communicating with you honestly and transparently.

While it's okay to say you've been upset or angry, you shouldn't show it. Raw emotions aren't helpful. And whatever you do, don't tell them you're "disappointed." They may already think they've

FINDING OUT WHAT'S WRONG

Here are a few suggested strategies for giving your child space to reveal what's worrying them.

1
I can tell something is making you unhappy; do you want to talk about it?

This can easily be deflected, but it establishes a tone.

2
I'm worried about you. Is it something online or in the real world?

Dividing your child's online and offline lives can help them judge the gravity of the problem. Pursue gently if they don't want to answer.

3
I love you, and I don't want to see you upset. I'm not going to be angry. What can I do to help?

Be sure that your facial expressions match what you're saying. Your child will notice if your words are calm but your face looks angry. If they don't answer, retreat, and let your words sink in.

4
If you want to talk, we can just keep it between us for now. Has someone asked you not to talk about it?

This helps reinforce the idea that you want to help your child rather than judge them. Explain to your child that secrets can be very dangerous.

5
Would you feel comfortable talking to _____ about it? No one will judge you; we just want to help. You don't have to deal with this alone.

If your child isn't comfortable talking to you, then provide options as to who else they can talk to. This will help take the weight off their shoulders.

let you down. Try to put yourself in their place. How would you want a parent to respond if you were the one in trouble?

The biggest risk your child can face is feeling that they are unable to talk to anyone about the problem. This is something predators deliberately try to engineer. If a child believes no one else will understand, then they won't seek help.

If your child won't talk to you, provide options of other people that they might feel comfortable talking to—mom/dad/sibling/cousin/aunt/grandparent/family friend. Even if they just talk to their friends, it's better than not confiding in anyone.

Also consider the possibility that someone might have asked your child to keep the problem a secret. Ask your child if this is the case, and explain that often when someone asks another person to keep a secret, they are doing so to protect themselves rather than the person they are asking. This is usually a serious warning sign that something bad might be developing.

WHAT DO I DO WHEN COMMUNICATION BREAKS DOWN?

If everything you've tried has failed and your child simply won't communicate with you, then you still need to keep yourself in check and not get angry. They may be in a dark place, and getting angry will only push them further into it.

Try to identify the source of their discomfort. When do they seem most upset? Is it when they return from school? When they've been on their device? Young children are often less capable of concealing their emotions or feelings. This makes the times when they're most upset easier to identify.

Once you've determined what might be a pattern—such as that they appear unhappy after using a particular app or site—then you need to take a robust approach: "Please tell me what's going on, or I'll have to remove this app or block this site." That may seem harsh—your child will certainly think so (prepare for tantrums)—but you're dealing with something, or someone, that clearly has a negative effect on them. Simply turning a blind eye isn't an option.

If the problem persists, you may have to consider an escalation strategy. That means telling your child that they have to speak to

NADIA:
The more troubled my girls seem, the more I try to engage with them on their level by talking about things such as what's trending on social media. I find this helps them open up.

NADIA:
I do think that a lot of parents agree with this advice, but in my experience, these sort of threats break down the trust between me and my girls.

KAYE:
I agree that continual threats to confiscate a phone will build animosity. However, if there is a breach of trust, or you are worried they might be in real trouble, you might have to do it anyway—even if you know it will cause an almighty row.

KAYE:
You can't always force a child to speak. Often, all you can do is sit them down in a room with someone else and hope that the problem comes out.

somebody, perhaps an older sibling or relative, or a family friend. The speaking bit is not up for negotiation.

If a family member isn't appropriate, you may need to involve a teacher or a doctor (especially if there are physical indicators, such as self-harm) or seek professional help from a suitable charity or counselor. In the most serious cases, you may need to involve the police. Seeking help from a third party isn't a failure. You're trying to do the best for your child, and everyone needs help sometimes.

WHAT SHOULD I DO IF MY CHILD BREAKS MY TRUST?

There may be times when your child deliberately and knowingly causes problems. This might include ignoring your instructions not to use a particular app, spending your money without permission, bullying other children online, or even continuing to speak to a suspicious online friend after you have told them not to.

In these circumstances, you need to consider the damage that your child could potentially do (or have done to them) if you don't take their device away. If you think the problem may get worse if you don't confiscate the device—because they don't understand what they are doing wrong, or they do understand but are continuing to do it anyway—you must take their device away until they regain your trust.

In less severe circumstances, an alternative to confiscating the phone (and a successful technique many of my clients have used with their children) is to delete apps from a child's phone one by one. For example, if a child is causing problems on a particular social media site, the parent can delete that app and then block the site on the child's online browser using the parental control options (see pp.212–215). The account would remain online, but the child wouldn't be able to access it. If the child continued to misbehave, more apps would be deleted, but if they managed to regain their parents' trust, then the apps would be redownloaded.

To ensure that strategy works, don't let your children know the app store password for their device or enable them to use fingerprint or face ID access for purchases, as this will enable them to redownload the app(s) you delete themselves.

TAKEAWAYS

1 BUILD TRUST BETWEEN YOU AND YOUR CHILD It is important that they know they can come to you with a problem.

2 TRY DIFFERENT METHODS OF COMMUNICATION Children will respond differently to different platforms and styles of conversation.

3 MAKE TIME TO TALK Reassure your child that there is always a good time for them to talk to you. Even if they might feel it is something silly or trivial, you'll find time to listen.

4 LOOK OUT FOR THE WARNING SIGNS Changes in your child's behavior can indicate that they are facing a problem.

5 OFFER YOUR CHILD OTHER PEOPLE TO TALK TO If communication breaks down between you and your child, there may be someone else they are willing to open up to.

6 STEP IN Take action if your gut tells you something is wrong or you notice your child is behaving significantly differently.

7 SECRETS CAN BE DANGEROUS Remind your child that a person asking them to keep a secret is probably doing so to protect themselves, not your child.

8 DON'T BE ANGRY OR DISAPPOINTED Even if you are, reacting in this way could make the situation worse.

9 BE CRUEL TO BE KIND Deleting an app or confiscating a device may feel mean, but it is often necessary to prevent further damage.

10 COMMUNICATE Maintain as much interest in your child's online world as their "real" world. Talk about what sites, games, and apps they like and don't like and who they talk to.

WANT MORE INFO? If this chapter hasn't answered all your questions, try:

- Creating a Healthy Tech Environment, pp.22–29
- Device Safety and Security, pp.200–217
- It's All Gone Wrong, pp.218–227

CREATING A HEALTHY TECH ENVIRONMENT

FOSTERING A POSITIVE RELATIONSHIP BETWEEN YOUR KIDS AND THEIR DEVICES

WHAT YOU NEED TO KNOW

NADIA'S EXPERIENCE

This topic quite literally makes me groan with despair! I don't ever sit chatting with a group of parents without it coming up within the hour.

How much screen time is the right amount of time? I have so many conflicting thoughts and feelings on this, as well as a healthy dose of guilt about the amount of time my husband and I spend staring into the black holes of our own phones. How can we guide our kids if we, too, are slaves?

Both my daughters are homeschooled, so evenings are very social for them as they catch up with all their friends who have been at school during the day. Let's face it: when I was a teen, I spent all my time on the equivalent social media platform in the 1970s and 1980s—it was called the landline!

Every night, they will spend hours FaceTiming, texting, and so on; and they are genuinely having a great time whenever I listen in—chatting, singing, dancing, and often being creative. I once overheard my eldest reading the whole of *Romeo and Juliet* to her boyfriend! I have to say, I loved that her first relationship was carried out predominantly on FaceTime in the safety of our home.

I have also been pleasantly surprised on those occasions. Having yelled, "What on earth are you doing on that phone again?" they have quickly corrected me and told me they are researching this or that subject. My kids have taught me an awful lot from what they have learned surfing the net. They are more engaged in politics and the world at large than I ever was at their age, and they certainly don't come in and flop down in front of the TV in the same way I used to when I was a kid!

But (and it's a big but), I also know they are absorbing a lot of negativity from their phones, and I often feel overwhelmed when trying to decide the right thing to do.

TEENAGERS in the US spend nearly **NINE HOURS** a day using entertainment media, including the **INTERNET**. Tweens **(AGED 8–12)** spend nearly **SIX HOURS** a day on similar screen time.

If I am truly honest, there have been many times when it has suited me for my children to be locked into their phones while I get on with what I need to do. And my kids are only too pleased to draw our attention to my husband's and my phone usage whenever we question theirs.

WILL'S EXPERT ANALYSIS

How many times do you look down at your phone every day, even when you haven't received an alert? According to a 2017 survey, the average American checks their phone 80 times a day—that's every 12 minutes!

Receiving text messages, comments on your social media posts, and emails often builds a sense of self-esteem, with each message alert triggering a short burst of happiness and even excitement. This leads to addiction, as people find themselves constantly returning to their devices to see if they'll get the next burst of positivity from someone making contact with them. Soon they crave this feeling and become depressed without it.

Every parent faces the same dilemma: you want your child to be a sociable, informed, and confident user of technology, but you don't want them to develop an unhealthy relationship with their devices and neglect the real world around them.

91% of **YOUNG PEOPLE** think they have a **HEALTHY RELATIONSHIP** with their **DEVICES.**

WILL'S CASE STUDY

ONLINE GAMING ADDICTION AT HOME LEADS TO TROUBLE AT SCHOOL

A client of mine gave her 10-year-old a tablet for his birthday and, despite encouraging him to use it for different things, found that he had been constantly playing a particular online game. Every time she took the device away for meal times, school, or when he had homework, the boy reacted extremely aggressively and angrily. She was seriously concerned that her previously quiet, mild-mannered child was behaving so aggressively. It wasn't just at home, either—she'd received calls from the school about his behavior there, too. She was at a loss as to what to do and needed my advice on how to treat his addiction.

79%
of **YOUNG**
people **KEEP** their
PHONE NEARBY
when they **SLEEP.**

WHAT ARE THE POTENTIAL PROBLEMS?

One or more of these issues could occur if your child has an unhealthy relationship with technology:

- **Distraction**—Various studies have found that children who frequently check their phones are more likely to become poor students. Even without their phones to attract their attention, many of the students in the study were constantly preoccupied by whether anyone was trying to contact them.
- **Impatience**—As technology gets faster, our patience gets shorter. We expect instant gratification all the time. A child who doesn't immediately get a lot of likes on social media might get agitated and check their page more frequently. The danger is that this impatience also manifests itself offline.
- **Self-esteem**—Social media often paints everyone else's lives as perfect, and your child may feel other people are always getting more likes than them. This can lead to a damaging obsession about their online appearance and popularity (see pp.54–56).
- **Isolation**—Some children find that they have more in common with their online friends than the children they meet in the real world. It's important that your child doesn't become so wrapped up in their online social life that they neglect their offline friends and find themselves isolated in the real world.
- **Underdeveloped social skills**—Communication via the Internet can be very different from speaking face to face. Children need enough offline communication to be able to develop those skills and recognize body language effectively.
- **Empathy**—Some people regularly insult or bully others online. If this is the majority of the social interaction your child encounters, they might think it is acceptable behavior.
- **Vision and hearing problems**—Excessive screen time can cause eyestrain, blurred vision, and dry eyes; while regularly listening to loud music can cause hearing problems, such as tinnitus (constant ringing in the ears) and hearing loss.
- **Neck and joint issues**—When you stand or sit upright, your head is supported by your spine. If you are tilting forward to look at a device, you're putting extra strain on your neck

muscles. This can lead to upper back pain and headaches. Gamers are also at risk of discomfort in their thumbs and wrists due to repetitive actions straining their tendons.

HOW CAN I CUT MY KIDS' SCREEN TIME?

I'm as bad as anyone when it comes to being distracted by my phone, so I've come up with four top tips to avoid being distracted. Encourage your kids to use them, as well as using them yourself:

- **Block more notifications.** There are many things your device will alert you to, but do you need to know about all of them immediately? I allow notifications to appear only when a person is communicating with me directly. For example, I allow text messages to appear but not social media posts.

- **Turn on "Do not disturb."** There are very few people who need to be contactable at all times—and your child certainly doesn't. Most connected devices have a "Do not disturb" mode that silences all incoming communications. In most cases, you can allow certain things to overrule this mode so your child doesn't miss a really important call. Turn this setting on overnight, and ensure that your child's phone isn't kept in their room while they're asleep—it's just too tempting!

- **Use the 30:60 rule.** Ideally, don't let your child use their device for longer than 30 minutes at a time. After 30 minutes, they should then spend 60 minutes doing something else—perhaps something active, such as going outside, doing chores, or having a face-to-face conversation. This will help avoid eye problems and repetitive strain injuries. Unless they're playing video games, watching television, or doing homework, there's probably not much they need to do online that takes more than 30 minutes. If they are gaming, try using a 60:60 minutes on:off ratio instead.

- **Turn on gray-scale mode.** Devices often have vivid color displays, and color can have a strong effect on your brain. If you remove the color, you may find that you check your phone much less frequently. The method of turning on gray-scale mode varies from phone to phone, so do an Internet search to find specific instructions for your model.

KAYE:
I find distraction is often a good way of limiting screen time. With my kids, their devices are their go-to when they have nothing to do. Making sure they have plenty of other interests and activities to occupy them automatically reduces screen time without causing any conflict.

TIMING IT

The 30:60-minute method isn't always possible to enforce. If you find this is the case, try one of the following tactics:

- Set an alarm for the amount of time you are happy for your child to use their device (e.g., for 1 hour if they're gaming). When you and your child hear the alarm go off, you can step in and ask your child to stop using their device.

- Use an app that allows you to set time limits for how long your child can use their device or when they can access certain games or apps.

IS THERE ANYTHING ELSE I CAN DO?

Yes, these are all more general strategies that will help ensure that your child has a healthy relationship with technology and that they are safe when using their device(s).

Stay safe when out and about

When you're out and about, you need be aware of your surroundings. You have five senses, and if your child is using a device with headphones, they are limiting two important senses: vision and hearing. A good rule of thumb is for your child to use devices only when standing still and not while walking or running.

In addition to limiting awareness, using a device while out and about makes your child a target—criminals could see a distracted child with a valuable device in their hand as an opportunity.

Set tech areas and enforce tech-free time

I'm a strong advocate of tech areas and tech-free time for a number of reasons. First, it's important for children to separate where is and isn't appropriate for them to use devices. If, for example, you have a rule that no one in the family can use their devices during dinnertime, then you can instill that boundary in your child.

Second, when children use their devices hidden away in their bedrooms or take their devices to the bathroom with them, you can't keep an eye on what they are doing and how long they are doing it for. This can become a big issue if your child spends a lot of time gaming alone in their room. If you do move your child's computer or game console to a family room, you can always get them headphones so that the rest of the family doesn't have to listen in to their game.

Finally, ensure that your child has a tech-free period of time before they go to bed. There's a growing body of research indicating that the blue light from devices' screens can affect our sleep and sleeping patterns. The current guidance is to avoid screen time for at least 1 hour before bedtime.

TEXTING AFTER LIGHTS OUT (even once a week) dramatically **INCREASES** reported **DAYTIME SLEEPINESS** among **TEENS**.

Set a good example

Make sure that you aren't doing any of the things that you encourage your kids not to do. This includes the advice in this chapter as well as that across the entire book. Children have a strong sense of fairness. If the rules apply to everybody, they'll be much easier to enforce.

TAKEAWAYS

1 LIMIT NOTIFICATIONS Allow notifications only for people contacting your child directly, and have periods of "do not disturb."

2 DO NOT DISTURB Ensure that your child doesn't keep their devices in their room overnight.

3 INSTIGATE TECH-FREE TIME This might be at the dinner table or for a set period of time before bed.

4 SET A TIME LIMIT Tell your child how long they have to use their device and stick to it. Impose the 30:60- or 60:60-minute rule, set a timer, or use an app that limits how long your child can use certain apps.

5 USE GRAY-SCALE MODE Removing the color display will make your child less likely to want to look at their phone.

6 DON'T LET YOUR CHILD USE THEIR PHONE WHILE WALKING Being distracted by a device makes your child vulnerable to accidents and criminals.

7 SET A GOOD EXAMPLE It's important to be seen to be practicing what you preach.

WANT MORE INFO If this chapter hasn't answered all your questions, try:

- Social Media, pp.46–65
- Device Safety and Security, pp.200–217
- It's All Gone Wrong, pp.218–227

CHATTING ONLINE

TEACHING YOUR CHILD ABOUT TALKING TO STRANGERS

WHAT YOU NEED TO KNOW

NADIA'S PERSPECTIVE

In the "good old days," being afraid for your child's safety in the adult world mostly involved thoughts of them being vulnerable when playing outside or walking home through dark streets. Boy, how things have changed! Now, of course, our children have the ability (using the very devices WE parents have bought them!) to invite the ENTIRE outside world into the safety and comfort of our own homes.

We had our first encounter of just how frightening this could be back when Maddie was just 9 years old, and her older half sister, Fleur, was visiting for the weekend.

It was a normal Saturday morning: Mark and I were getting on with chores, the girls were happily playing on Mark's laptop, and Fleur was full of the excitement at having just signed up to a brilliant social media site—Facebook. We believed Facebook was a safe haven for the girls to sit and look at photos, and Mark had all manner of security systems on his laptop, so we thought all would be safe—how wrong we were!

As I was vacuuming downstairs (a very rare occurrence), I could hear the girls giggling and having a good time. I was a happy mama! Then, all of a sudden, the sound of laughter gave way to spine-chilling shrieks and crying, followed by Maddie running into her room and poor Fleur coming hurtling down the stairs looking horrified.

Once we'd calmed the poor things down, we discovered that, while innocently perusing Fleur's Facebook page, a friend of Fleur's had shared a link to a "fun" chat room all about bunny rabbits and seemingly catering to young girls. When they innocently clicked through on the link, they arrived at a chat room that seemed to be fun enough, until four men appeared and started chatting to them telling them they were pretty. As they started to

As many as

43%

of **CHILDREN** have spoken to a **STRANGER ONLINE.**

have second thoughts, they described seeing the "live" process of a man getting his penis out and—well, we don't need to explain what it was that he was doing.

Maddie was in a flood of tears, and, although she says she only just saw things very briefly before Fleur closed the laptop, she was deeply upset for a long time afterward. She still refers to the incident even now—six years later. It freaks me out that what actually happened right here in our very own house with both my husband and myself in the vicinity was tantamount to child sex abuse via social media—truly terrifying.

WILL'S EXPERT ANALYSIS

Our parents warned us not to speak to strangers, but it seems that virtually every app is telling our children the opposite. Children use their devices to communicate in a dazzling variety of ways: instant messaging, online forums, social media comments, live video broadcasting, and online gaming (to name just a few). They may have entirely different groups of real and online friends on different services, as shown below.

Even younger children, who might not have their own phone, often have access to a parent or older sibling's tablet or computer. Many games have a built-in chat function, and this can be a child's

On average, **CHILDREN** aged 11–15 spend

of their **TIME ONLINE COMMUNICATING** with other people.

WILL'S CASE STUDY

EXPLICIT MESSAGES SENT TO YOUNG ONLINE GAMER BY ADULT PLAYERS

A very distressed parent got in contact with me. They had gone on their child's gaming console to install a new game as a surprise for their 8-year-old child and noticed there were lots of messages from other gamers stored on it. Curiosity drove them to look at the messages, some of which were written messages and others were audio recordings. The content was explicit, and it was clear from the voice that the speaker was a grown man.

first introduction to chatting with strangers. Sadly, stranger danger is a problem online as much as it is in the real world, and this is something children need to be aware of.

How big is the problem?

Children of all ages chat online. When safe and supervised, this is great, but unfortunately it's sometimes hard to monitor online chat, so it's a fantastic tool for predators. Law enforcement organizations around the world warn that online chatting platforms, such as those listed above, are playgrounds for predators. As many as 43 percent of 8- to 16-year-olds say that they've spoken to a stranger online, and 69 percent of teenagers report being contacted regularly by strangers and not telling their parents or guardians. So it's essential that you know what apps and sites your child uses and what sort of things people are talking to them about.

How could it affect your family?

There's the risk that your child will be given bad information or fed opinions that could influence how they act or treat people. They might be tricked into doing things by people pretending to be another child—scammed into buying expensive items they don't need, pressured into doing something dangerous, or even recorded doing something that can later be used against them for blackmail.

Your child might watch or chat about live broadcasts of things that initially seem quite innocent but that turn into something graphic, or even dark and twisted—such as live stunts that have gone wrong or even criminals broadcasting their crimes.

Beyond the direct impact to your child, there's also the risk of them sharing too much information—who they are, where they live, which school they go to, their siblings' names, and so on, all of which makes them, and others, vulnerable to predators (see p.36).

How can you prevent it from happening?

Talking to your child is one of the best ways to prevent any issue. Let your child know that you trust them and that they can and should tell you about anything they see online that upsets them.

THE RULES FOR ONLINE CHATTING

Ensuring that your kids stick to these rules will help keep them safe while chatting online.

- Only use sites you, the parent, know are safe and are happy for them to use.

- Never log into a website using an account from a social media website (for example, a Facebook account) because this gives others potential access to their social media.

- Never agree to take a conversation somewhere else (for example, to another site or app, or to email, text, or phone).

- Never click on any links inside messages from someone they don't know—they could be viruses or horrible photos.

- Be suspicious of what people say online—they may not be telling the truth.

- Leave a site right away if someone makes them uncomfortable.

- Tell you or a trusted adult if they see or experience something nasty or scary.

Tell your child that they should be cautious about people they meet online. Explain that people don't always tell the truth, so they should automatically be wary of strangers. Give them a set of rules for chatting online (see left)—and make sure that they stick to them.

Keep track of which sites or services your child uses (you can do this with your child). Check the sorts of content and comments being posted on them, or look for online reviews of the sites to find out whether other people have experienced problems.

What should you do if it's already happened?

It is possible for kids to accidentally end up somewhere they didn't intend to be. If your child has already encountered suspicious, aggressive, or disturbing behavior while using an online chatting service, either block the perpetrator or gather evidence of their actions and report them to the site administrators using the "Help" or "Contact Us" links (often at the very top or very bottom of the web page). Site administrators make sure that no one is doing anything nasty in an online forum, game, or comment feed and will be able to ban users who are breaking the site's rules.

If your child has used a site or app you've told them not to, or if they've broken the rules (see box, left), impose limitations on when and how they can use their device(s) (see p.20), or take their device(s) away until you can trust them. Make sure that you explain to your child why you are doing this and why what they were doing was dangerous.

> **NADIA:**
> I'd never confiscate my teenager's phone. I think this would just destroy the trust she has in me.

When should you seek outside help?

If your child has been targeted by a person or group, you need to change their username (the public name they use on a site or instant messaging service; see p.36) and report the users who have been targeting your child to the site administrators or app provider. If you think the behavior is illegal, take screenshots or photos of the offending messages and give them to the police. See pp.226–227 for guidance on how to gather evidence. If necessary, delete the accounts altogether.

> **WILL:**
> Trust needs to work both ways, though, and I believe this has to be established at an early age. If you don't want to confiscate their phone, try deleting their apps one by one (see p.20).

PARENTS' QUESTIONS ANSWERED

I know I can't stop my kids from chatting online, but how can I make sure they're safe?

TOP THINGS NOT TO SHARE ONLINE

Make sure that your child knows not to share these pieces of information with online friends or strangers:

- Their real name
- Their location or home address
- Their school, clubs, or sports teams
- Places they regularly visit with friends or family
- Names of family members
- Date of birth
- Passwords
- Email addresses
- Telephone numbers
- Their other online accounts and usernames (e.g., social media or online gaming)

Regularly remind your child that a friend who they've only ever met online should always be treated with suspicion: there's no way of knowing whether they are who they say they are.

How can I or my child tell who they are really chatting with?

You can't, but what you can do is try to find out more about them and check this information against an online search. For example, an online friend might say that they're a fan of the same football team as your child. Are there questions your child can ask that only a real fan would know the answers to? This isn't foolproof—the other person can Google the answers, or they may be a genuine football fan who is using a fake identity; however, asking questions may give you or your child a sense of whether or not someone is acting suspiciously.

Why do people need to use a nickname, and what is a good one to have?

Although nicknames hide others' identities, they are a sensible way to keep your child's real identity hidden online—for example, love_unicorns301 from Oxford is a lot harder to track than KatieSmith35. Nicknames should be unique and free from identifiable information, such as the year of birth, the name of a pet or school, or anything else that might help others locate your child. Avoid provocative nicknames, too, such as BabyGirl123 or HandsomeBoy445.

How can I spot if a conversation has turned sinister?

Children don't tend to ask the same questions as adults; they want to know how you complete a level of a game, not what street you live on. Someone who starts a conversation by asking about age, gender, and location (often shortened to "ASL?") is someone to be suspicious of. If they follow up with further questions, such as "Where are your parents?" or there is the hint of anything offensive in their conversation, it's unlikely that your child is talking to another child.

Is anyone from the websites themselves checking these forum and chat room sites?

Sometimes—sites may have administrators ("admins") or moderators ("mods"), who are there to keep an eye on a chat room to make sure that people aren't being nasty or doing things they shouldn't. They may only look in on conversations every now and again, so don't assume they will step in as soon as there is a problem.

If your child experiences anything unpleasant, contact the site administrators first, as this can help them ban users who misbehave. This also goes for forums and message boards, although administrators can be slower to respond on these platforms. Not all sites will have administrators, so try to make sure your child sticks to those that do.

An incredible

86%

of **GIRLS** claimed they had **ONLINE CHATS** that their **PARENTS DIDN'T KNOW** about.

What are private areas of a chat room?

Many chat rooms and message services, such as WhatsApp, have the digital equivalent of private rooms, which are spaces into which one user can invite another user to carry out conversations without admins seeing what they are saying. Your child should avoid a private chat invite from users they know only online.

> **My daughter likes webcam chatting with her online friends. People can't get any personal information from that, can they?**

10%

of **CHILDREN** aged 12–15 have **BROADCAST LIVE VIDEO** material of **THEMSELVES.**

They can get a lot. Before your child posts any photo or video, think very carefully about who can view it, what your child is wearing, and what viewers can see behind your child.

Many professional vloggers (video bloggers) record their posts in front of a plain or computer-generated background. That's not just to make the viewers focus on them; it's also because they don't want to give away any identifiable information about their location and offline life. These vloggers recognize that not all of their viewers are necessarily nice, well-intentioned people.

HOW TO AVOID OVERSHARING ON A WEBCAM

Before allowing your child to use a webcam, check that they aren't giving away too much about themselves.

This picture shows what a predator could use to make conversation or locate your child.

1 Lives near a church or obvious landmark

2 Fan of a particular band or celebrity

3 Good at sports

4 Plays a musical instrument

5 Goes to a particular school

6 Device model, PIN code visible if typed in

7 Enjoys reading or a specific book

What can they pick up about my daughter's location from her surroundings?

We give a lot of information away when we photograph or film outside. Landmarks, street signs, buses with numbers on them, and many more things can make it surprisingly easy to work out where somebody is.

There are indoor clues, too. A school uniform or sweatshirt in the background may tell viewers what school your child goes to, while posters of bands or sports teams give away your child's interests. Check whether these things become visible if the camera pans around from its original position. The reason you need to think about this is because someone may see something of interest in the background and steer the conversation toward it. "Do you like X singer?" That can help them "socially engineer" your child (see p.103). You and your child should check for all of these clues on-screen before posting any webcam photos or videos (see box, below).

A neutral background removes clues to your child's interests and location. Before going online, make sure:

1 Blinds are closed to hide location and time of day

2 No posters reveal favorite bands, celebrities, or sports team

3 No objects are visible to reveal personal interests

4 Clothes are plain and neutral

5 Desk is empty so phone messages/ PIN code can't be seen, and no other devices are visible

6 No photos of family or friends are visible anywhere in the room

Can anyone take an image from my child's video? Or can they use her camera without her knowing?

Yes, you can take a screenshot of anything that appears on your screen—including a video of someone else. People can then zoom in on even the smallest details of the image to try to gain more information. Some apps tell you if someone takes a screenshot of your post, but don't rely on this.

The risk of a hacker actually taking over your child's camera and switching it on without her knowing is more remote, but it does occasionally happen. Covering the camera lens when she's not using it, for example, with a peelable sticker, is an easy and effective solution to avoid this possibility.

My son doesn't use chat sites, but he does play a lot of online games. Should I be worried about who he's talking to?

Potentially, yes. Many games have a microphone option so players can communicate with each other. This often exposes children to bad language, which is seen as part of the hustle and bustle of gaming but can upset younger children—and older children should be told not to do this to others. Bullying is also a problem, especially for girls or children from minority groups and particularly on associated sites, such as gaming discussion forums or live game-streaming sites, such as Twitch.

He's been asked to share a video game "mod"— should he?

Sharing mods (homemade video game modifications that alter aspects of the game, not to be confused with the mods who moderate online spaces) or cheats (such as extra lives) is part and parcel of gaming culture, but it's something that shouldn't happen outside the game itself because it might require giving out an email address or other identifying information. I'd also advise your child not to buy mods or cheats from other players and for you to keep an eye on your credit card—in one case, a 7-year-old boy spent nearly $5,000 on mods and cheats he'd been encouraged to buy.

KAYE:
How can I make sure my kids can't use my credit cards without asking me first?

WILL:
Make sure that a password is required for all purchases and in-app purchases (see pp.216–217) and don't tell your kids the password for any online accounts that your credit card is attached to (e.g., Amazon).

Do pedophiles or con artists target gamers specifically, or is there a typical profile of a user who is targeted?

This is a big problem. For most mainstream gaming console networks, users have to provide their credit card details to access online servers so people can't sign up pretending to be somebody else. However, nonconsole gaming networks (app- or laptop-based) can be more treacherous. These are often run by smaller companies who don't have the resources to police their games in the same way. The best thing you can do is regularly monitor which games your child plays (whether on a console, computer, tablet, or smartphone) and the online interactions your child has with other users while playing. This will allow you to step in if you are concerned.

How would he block or report someone who has turned nasty?

All the major consoles and games have a way to block, mute, or report other players. Gaming is a big-money business, and they have a vested interest in keeping players safe.

He always uses headphones—is there a problem with this?

For many families, headphones are a blessing; otherwise, you'd hear every sound in the game. However, most consoles enable users to talk while they play, so if your child uses headphones, it may be wise to listen in from time to time.

79%

of **CHILDREN** aged 12–15 and as many as **69%** of children aged 8–11 **PLAY VIDEO GAMES ONLINE.**

He has lots of online friends, and he's talking about meeting one of them in real life. Is that a good idea?

You need to think very carefully about this. If you decide that you are happy for your son to meet his online friend, then make sure that he does so somewhere public and goes with you or another trusted adult. That adult should then stay with him the entire time.

My daughter's gay, and I know she uses LGBT forums, but I'm really worried about who else is on them.

LGBT (lesbian, gay, bisexual, or trans) sites have been brilliant for LGBT people, especially if they regularly experience prejudice due to their sexuality or gender identity. The Internet can offer reassurance that they're not alone. Some LGBT people don't use these sites to date but simply to find like-minded people to chat to. This isn't just true for LGBT kids; many children who feel isolated in the real world find their niche in an online community. Your daughter may be comfortable on these sites because she feels people on them won't judge her or that they have relevant advice to share.

Sadly, these forums also attract bad people and can be used to commit various hate crimes. LGBT kids can be uniquely vulnerable. They might have been rejected or feel isolated at home or at school due to their sexuality or gender identity and so are more likely to trust like-minded people online, or they might be targeted by those looking to identify and harm LGBT people. There have been terrible cases of assaults committed by people using dating apps and sites to identify and attack LGBT people in this manner.

That's terrifying. Should I tell her to stop?

No, but your daughter does need to be conscious of the people who might try to harm her: the trolls, the bullies, or worse. Look at the site she's using—is it safe? Can anybody post there with little or no verification? Are there controls to protect against threats or report worrying behavior? Does it have moderators (see p.37)? Can you block others?

If you can't be sure, try working with her to find sites that are safer, age appropriate, and suitable for what she wants to do. Online reviews of specific sites may tell you whether other people have found them safe or if they have encountered any problems while using them.

> My daughter doesn't use dating sites—she's a bit too young for that—but she still gets guys trying to chat her up on pretty much every kind of website.

It's sad but true that women's and girls' experiences of the Internet are very different to that of most men and boys. Every girl is going to experience unsolicited and often unwelcome attention from men in the real world and online.

Is there anything I can do to stop this?

It's really important to talk to your daughter and help her understand what the boundaries are—what she shouldn't have to tolerate—and it's equally important for the parents of boys to have similar conversations with their child about what is and isn't acceptable. This upfront guidance removes a great deal of confusion and uncertainty.

On a practical level, she needs to make sure that if a conversation makes her feel uncomfortable, she logs off and leaves the site or app on which it is happening.

NADIA:
I say to my girls that they must listen to their instinct and tell me or their dad if something feels wrong. We won't be cross, and we will always try to help.

43

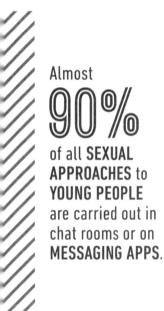

Almost **90%** of all **SEXUAL APPROACHES** to **YOUNG PEOPLE** are carried out in chat rooms or on **MESSAGING APPS**.

What can she do about someone who is persistent?

Most social media platforms have tools she can use to temporarily silence or permanently block other users. They usually also have reporting systems through which your daughter can notify the website administrators of anybody sending explicit or distressing messages or media.

If there's no means to mute, block, or report abusive behavior, she should tell the perpetrators that she is underage, that they are breaking the law, and that, if they continue, she will report them to the site admins and the authorities—do they want a visit from the police? Ideally, encourage her not to use the site in the future. Sometimes the best policy is just to find a different site that does a better job of providing a safe space for everybody who is using it.

TAKEAWAYS

1 BE AWARE OF THE DANGERS Forewarn your child about the inappropriate language or opinions they might encounter.

2 KEEP TALKING Maintain trust so that your child comes to you about online friends and experiences.

3 ENCOURAGE SAFE CHATTING Make sure your kids stick to the rules for chatting online (see p.34).

4 READ SITE REVIEWS Do your research so you can weed out poorly regulated sites.

5 CHECK FOR GIVEAWAYS Make sure no background webcam details reveal personal information that predators can use to "socially engineer" your child.

6 WATCH OUT FOR PREDATORS Keep an eye on conversations and alert your child to suspicious signs, such as someone asking for personal details or wanting to move the chat to a private forum.

7 REPORT PERSISTENT NUISANCE BEHAVIOR Before your child leaves a site that they feel uncomfortable with, screenshot any evidence and report the perpetrator to the site admins or, if serious, the police—you could be protecting other kids as well as your own.

8 GET TO KNOW THEIR FRIENDS Talk to your child about who they talk to or play online games with.

9 TAKE CARE MEETING VIRTUAL FRIENDS Tell your child that they must tell you if they ever want to meet an online friend. Make sure that they are with an adult the entire time.

WANT MORE INFO? If this chapter hasn't answered all your questions, try:

- Cyberbullying and Trolls, pp.68–71
- Grooming, pp.98–101
- Coercion, Extortion, and Blackmail, pp.136–139

SOCIAL MEDIA

WHAT YOUR CHILD IS VIEWING AND POSTING ON THEIR FAVORITE NETWORKING SITES

WHAT YOU NEED TO KNOW

13 is the **MINIMUM AGE** set by most **SOCIAL MEDIA SITES** for users, However, very **FEW SITES** actually ask users to **VERIFY** their **AGE** before creating a new account.

KAYE'S EXPERIENCE

Social media keeps me awake at night. I worry about all the harm it might be doing to my children. They might be bullied or groomed, stalked or trolled, or exposed to porn and violence. Their brains might shrink to the size of a pea because of all the dumb stuff on it, and they might become horribly unfit by devoting all their energy to liking and sharing rather than running and jumping. They might even lose the ability to write in full sentences and only be able to communicate in emoji-speak.

That's my doomsday scenario—the nightmare I torture myself with. And I have to concede: it makes me somewhat irrational. There are times I catch them looking at their phones (which is almost every conscious moment), and I just randomly blurt out: "Get off that social media!"

I don't even always know they are *on* social media; I just make an automatic assumption, and it is so annoying when they smugly show me their screen to reveal that they are actually discussing math homework in a group chat. I slink away like a wounded animal...

Social media *can* have a whole host of negative impacts, but as a mom to two adolescent daughters, I am trying to get things in perspective and not always see it as a big scary monster. Both Nadia and I use Twitter, Instagram, and Facebook, and our experience has been largely positive. In the digital world, as in the "real world," we've found that the good people far, far outnumber the bad.

But... there's always a but... you need to learn the rules of the digital road and ask questions. What platforms does your child use? What's the attraction? What are they doing? Who are they interacting with? Establishing those facts is always a good start. My eldest, like so many teenagers, is a slave to Snapchat. She has a Facebook profile but rarely posts—same for Instagram.

So, my worries?

Definitely exposure to enhanced and unrealistic images and how it affects her self-esteem: we've had long chats about that. We've also discussed what a "friend" really is and how you decide who you can and can't trust with your feelings and your personal information. The language we employ is a big concern for me, too. An ill-thought-out, throwaway comment can really wound and damage relationships with friends. With social media, you can't always assume that your child is going to be the victim, either. Inexperience, immaturity, raging hormones, and the relative anonymity of a keyboard can bring out the worst in anyone.

But parents need to learn, too. Check your social media. If someone were to look over your posts with all the pictures and the details about your daily routine and your travels, how much information would they be able to glean about *your* family's life?

Nearly **1/4** of all 8- TO 11- year-old children **HAVE a SOCIAL MEDIA PROFILE.**

WILL'S EXPERT ANALYSIS

So many children use multiple social media accounts, but in having multiple accounts, they're increasing the risks to themselves. Someone might hijack one of their accounts, give them fake information, encourage them to do dangerous or inappropriate online dares (as in the case below), or commit hate crimes—there are many ways social media exposes kids to danger.

WILL'S CASE STUDY

CHILD ALMOST DIES DOING ONLINE CHALLENGE

A parent told me about how their son had run into the kitchen with his face bright red, his eyes watering, and his mouth stuffed with cotton balls. Unable to breathe, he clawed at his mother for help. She started to pull the cotton balls out, but it was incredibly difficult because the boy's saliva had made them stick together. When she had removed the cotton balls, she asked her son what on earth he was thinking, stuffing cotton balls into his mouth. He said he'd been doing the "Chubby Bunny" online challenge, where people fill their mouths with marshmallows. He didn't have any marshmallows, so he used cotton balls instead. His parents were terrified he'd have suffocated if they hadn't been around to help.

How big is the problem?

There are billions of people using social media sites across the world. Potentially all of those people have the ability to access, copy, and repost everything your child puts online if your child doesn't have their security settings set up correctly. You never know where something might end up.

SOCIAL MEDIA RESCUE

Use this checklist to help you detect and deal with social media abuses such as bullying and harassment.

● Check your child's device, keep a note of which apps they use, and search their Internet history to identify all their accounts and activity.

● If a particular online group is upsetting your child, get your child to leave the group and ideally delete the account.

● If the problem is with one person, block them if you can and report them to the site.

● If the problem is an image or message, delete it if possible or report it. Note who you contact at the site and when. Social media sites can be slow to respond so keep trying until you get a result.

● If you want to check that an image has been removed, type "/?" at the end of the Internet address in the browser bar. Adding this to the site address ensures that you see the most up-to-date version of a page.

How could it affect your family?

Many kids will spend more time using social media than any other aspect of the Internet. There are lots of positives to social media, but while it can educate and inform, it can also mislead, harm, and even lead to criminal offenses if someone abuses a child online.

Social media takes advantage of children's natural desire for approval and anxiety about being left out. Regular notifications about other people's posts gives a sense that there is always something happening online, so your child can start to feel that they have to be checking social media sites all the time to avoid missing out. Facebook's first president, Sean Parker, admitted that the main goal of the site was to attract and hold people's attention. The sense of excitement at getting likes on one post fuels a desire to post more content and get more likes. He says, "It's a social-validation feedback loop.... It's exploiting a vulnerability in human psychology."

Some sites focus on people looking strong or sexy, which can have a negative impact on a child's body image and self-esteem. Even adults can sometimes find it hard to remember that what they see online is a heavily edited version of someone's appearance.

Social media also exposes your child to advertising, much of it targeted at younger users. The constant reminder of products children want but can't afford to buy can become overwhelming and even influence children to spend all of their (or your) money.

Finally, social media can be a platform on which issues such as cyberbullying (see pp.68–71) and cyberstalking (see pp.84–87) take place or provide a means for children to share compromising images of other children (see pp.117–118). Children may even post compromising material themselves (see pp.119–120).

How can you prevent it from happening?

Ask your child which social media sites or apps they use, what's good about them, and what isn't so good. Check the minimum age for these sites. If your child is too young, explain that age limits are there for their safety, even if "everybody is using it." There's usually an alternative they can sign up to.

You might want to consider not using your child's full name when setting up their social media account (e.g., Tom R) and providing an emoji or cartoon instead of a profile picture. This will reduce their digital footprint (see pp.192–199).

Check that location sharing is disabled in their device's Settings menu for the app or site that they're using (see p.207). This will help you ensure that, if they do get approached by a predator, they aren't revealing their whereabouts to them.

If your children are still relatively young but have social media accounts, you should know their usernames and passwords. Set their account email address and two-factor authentification (see p.205) as your own email address and phone number. This means they can't change their logins without you knowing.

What should you do if it's already happened?

Ask your child questions—what you know already might just be the tip of the iceberg. The priority is for you to gain control and recover the situation. Follow the advice in the box, left, and if your child's account does need to be taken down, then make sure they understand the serious reasons for it. You don't want your child to interpret the curtailing of their online social life as a punishment.

When should you seek outside help?

Your child may encounter bullying or peer pressure on social media sites, and these can sometimes be solved by talking to the others involved, blocking the offender, or notifying the site admins. You may want to get the police involved if your child has posted a compromising picture or message, if they have been approached by somebody who may be a predator, or if they have been seriously threatened, harassed, bullied, or stalked (see pp.220–221).

NADIA:
Whoops! I'm embarrassed to say that I do allow my underage children to use these apps. I just keep an open dialogue with them about the dangers.

KAYE:
I think age limits on social media sites are a sham—the sites are aware they have many underage users and make no attempt to police them. In any case, I'd rather know my girls are on a site than kid myself they aren't.

WILL:
You both make good points, but age limits are there for a reason: to protect users. Ignoring them could expose your children to unsuitable content. The key is knowing where your kids are, what they're saying, and what they're seeing.

PARENTS' QUESTIONS ANSWERED

My son seems obsessed with his social media status— the likes and followers. Is it really about social gratification?

It is. When we post a picture, we want our friends to not only see it but also demonstrably show that they like it. For children who are still determining who they are and where they fit in with their peer groups, this is significant. Are their friends getting more "likes" than they are? Are they getting complimentary comments on their pictures? There's a very strong competitive pull, too, and the more positives they get, the more their self-esteem is boosted; conversely, the fewer they get, the worse they feel.

He's got 5,000 followers—he can't know that many people? Who are they?

He is unlikely to know that many people personally. There's a lot of competition between children on how many friends they have on their social media pages; it's a mark of their popularity and status, and celebrities and social "influencers" encourage this. The danger in accepting any and every request to amass friends and followers is that they may give a stranger (or even predator) access to all their posts and online information. This, of course, applies to parents, too, and all the information they share online about their kids.

Followers and friends can also be bought, and there are dedicated websites devoted to this. Check his page to see if he's suddenly acquired a vast number overnight, or look at

52%
of **TEENS** on Facebook hit "**LIKE**" at least once **EVERY** single **DAY**.

your credit card history to see if he's "bought" friends. Some of these bought friends may be real people, but most are likely to be automation services, bots, "zombie" (inactive) accounts, or artificially created "fake friends," which is a potentially more insidious possibility because these could have been set up for the purposes of grooming or scamming (see also p.99 and p.137).

How can you determine whether a follower is a bot or "fake friend"?

Look at the postings on the friend's page—if they are up-to-date and reasonably frequent (they have a high level of engagement), and the comments are personality-based and individual, they are more likely to be real. Read their profile thoroughly—does it seem exaggerated or simply not true?

SPOTTING THE BOT

Read the telltale signs that a social media profile isn't all it seems. The following could indicate that the person you're befriending is either a fake or a "bot."

1 Perfect-looking profile picture—this could have been lifted from Google images.

2 First name only.

3 Has very low number of followers but follows lots of people.

4 Either an exaggerated or a vague profile.

5 All their posts are reposted from other people.

6 Not many likes on posts.

7 Not many comments on posts.

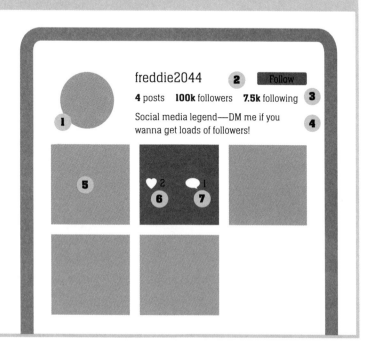

NADIA:
How do I search the Internet for an image, Will?

WILL:
Right-click on the image and select "copy image address/url." Then go to the Google image search website and click on the camera icon in the search bar. Now paste the image link into the search bar and press "Search by image."

Does their profile picture seem genuine? Try doing an image search of their profile picture to see if it's copied from another site. If you're not sure someone is friendly, your child should ask them some detailed questions (see p.36).

Is his privacy being compromised by having so many friends and followers?

Quite simply, yes. No matter how secure your son's privacy settings are set, as soon as he accepts a friend request, that person then has access to everything that he posts as well as to all of his previous posts. If he is going to accept requests from people he doesn't know, he has made a public account.

Worse than that, your son's friends are also likely to accept this person if they see your son is friends with them—your son has essentially validated this person as a real friend. And then the pool can grow even wider, with your son's friends' friends accepting the person. This means that your son may be helping an imposter gain access to the posts of everyone within his immediate social group and beyond.

My daughter is taking incessant selfies and has become obsessed about what she looks like. Is that healthy?

Selfies are a sign of the times: we all want to look good in photographs, and technology enables us to take a whole bunch of photos and pick out the one that shows us at our best. Where, in the past, we might have experimented with hair or makeup and taken a handful of Polaroid pictures, children today like to see how they look in their smartphone camera apps using various filters or makeup tricks they've picked up online. As their body changes, taking photos can be a way for them to map things, to see how far they've come. It's only when things become negative, compromising, or perhaps obsessive that it's something to worry about.

Why does it matter so much to her?

It could be self-esteem issues, the "power of likes", or the fact that the opinion of a teenager's peer group matters more to them than their family's. Our kids probably won't even settle for being told they're beautiful by their real friends; they want to know their online friends think they look good, too.

Within certain parameters, this is absolutely fine. The issue is more about whether the constant selfies are making your daughter unhappy with who she is. Try to get to the motivation behind it. Is she competing with her peers, trying to attract a specific person or group, or just attempting to boost her confidence?

What are the warning signs of something more ominous?

Keep a close eye on your daughter's behavior. Does she seem happy, or is she frustrated? Does taking selfies seem to make her depressed, anxious, agitated, or overly self-critical? If these signs are evident, there could be more deep-rooted issues for what is motivating her. The same peer approval all children seek can easily turn negative. For example, your daughter may have been rejected by somebody she fancied or teased about her appearance or a physical feature by others but is still taking selfies in the bid for approval.

Also keep an eye on whether her appearance has changed or is out of character—is she suddenly wearing more makeup than usual and/or oversexualizing her image? Some of this may just be about growing up and be part of expressing who she is, but is it possible she is creating a more sophisticated image to increase her number of likes? Or is it an attempt to attract someone in particular?

NADIA:
It makes me sad my daughter has body issues, and she says she has been greatly influenced by social media. I don't always have the answers, but I will always listen.

KAYE:
Yes, despite all I've tried, my eldest still mournfully shows me photos of airbrushed "pretty" girls. At a certain age, kids' friends just have more influence on them than their parents. A silent hug is often the best I can offer.

How can I make her more skeptical of the "perfect" images she is seeing on social media sites?

Explain that even beauty bloggers admit that their photos look good because of the careful lighting, posing, and makeup they use. Celebrities spend thousands of dollars on photographers and stylists, and then the images are digitally edited afterward. A huge amount of time, money, and work goes into that "just got out of bed" natural look. Make sure your daughter knows that no one can compete with that and that she shouldn't measure herself against an ideal that doesn't exist in real life.

You could show her videos teaching the tricks of the trade in professional photography and explain to her that, for some people, editing their own image can become something of an obsession. Once she knows the tricks, they're hard to miss, and seeing the process may help demystify for her how celebrities manage to look good all the time. If none of this seems to work, it may be worth approaching a professional counselor to speak to your daughter.

KAYE:
I'd be wary of doing this with older kids—my girls know all the makeup and lighting tricks better than I do!

WILL:
Yes, maybe best to target this at younger kids before they get too "savvy."

It's easy to get really worried when you read about sites telling kids how to hide anorexia, bulimia, self-harm, and things like that from their parents. Is there a way to keep our kids away from that stuff?

Thankfully, many Internet search engines are beginning to clean up and close down many "ana" (anorexia) and "mia" (bulimia) sites, but there are still more out there on the web that are easy enough to find if your child wants to search for them. These groups aren't just on the traditional World Wide Web, either—some of the most disturbing ana/mia groups are on phone-to-phone instant-messaging apps, which makes finding them exceptionally difficult, even for the police. Hopefully this means they will be difficult for your kids to find, too.

It doesn't help that the lines between healthy eating and eating disorders can become very blurry on social media—particularly on the image-driven social media sites kids favor.

Is there a way to block these sites?

Only to an extent. Parental control software or services enable you to block certain keywords and the Internet addresses that are known to be dangerous or dodgy, but they can't necessarily do the same as easily on messaging apps—and they can't possibly know about all the different websites, forums, blogs, boards, and other platforms where these conversations happen. Many messenger apps, such as WhatsApp, have desktop or web browser versions that enable you to see all of the conversations that have happened on the phone. You may want to use these to see what groups your child has joined (see p.214).

Blocking such content is incredibly difficult. If you type "thin and beautiful" into Google, you can come up with images of "inspiring" but often skeletal figures; typing "how to hide weight loss from parents" can bring up pro-eating-disorder discussion groups. These are good examples of the problem: many sites claim to be about support and recovery from eating disorders but are full of people offering advice on how to hide the signs of their disorder, not how to recover from it.

The good news is that the Internet can also help. The organizations listed at the back of the book provide really good advice for children and families, as do many reputable health websites (see p.232).

CHILDREN NOW SPEND MORE TIME ONLINE than they do **WATCHING TV.** For **9- TO 17-** year-olds, most of that time is spent using **SOCIAL MEDIA.**

I heard my son talking about doing one of those stupid social media challenges. He was actually going to try to dislocate his thumb!

That's one of the worst social media challenges I've seen. It started off with somebody sharing an image from a medical site and explaining, step by step, how to dislocate your thumb, shrugging off questions as to whether it hurt; it ended up with hundreds of children deliberately dislocating their thumbs and uploading the footage for their friends to see.

Like all of these crazes, it takes only a few social media "influencers"—people who have huge online audiences—to persuade lots of people to do silly or even dangerous things. These crazes are all about the reaction you get from your peers (online or offline) or the number of followers you can gain when you do something "incredible" on the Internet.

Foolish dares have always been part of playground culture. Isn't this the same thing?

Yes and no. The difference is that some of the crazes are actually dangerous in a way playground crazes don't tend to be: few die from following through a playground bet, but people have died from doing social media challenges, and many have been hospitalized. While in the past, bets and challenges between friends were contained to that friendship group, today ill-advised ideas can be quickly spread around the world to like-minded daredevils. In recent years, teenagers have dared each other to do various dangerous things, such as burning their skin with ice or eating poisonous laundry detergent capsules. In many parts of the world, the pressure to create ever more dangerous selfies, such as on train tracks or on top of cliffs or buildings, has seen many teenagers suffer terrible injuries or even die.

22%
of **TEENS** log onto their favorite **SOCIAL MEDIA** site more than **10 TIMES EVERY DAY**.

How do I stop him from doing something stupid?

The key is in how you can reframe your son's thinking and
motivation so he's not tempted to try anything dangerous.
Explain how you see him as a smart young adult and that
smart young adults wouldn't do something so dangerous.

Unfortunately, the more stupid or dangerous something
is, the more tempting it is to try—not least because of peer
pressure and the desire to be the most daring member of
your group. Crazes often escalate because people get bored,
so what attracted lots of likes one day may be old news
the next.

> **NADIA:**
> This sounds like good advice to me!

> **KAYE:**
> Although I'd be careful not to make your son feel bad if he had done something stupid. He might feel embarrassed already, and I find crushing kids further for doing something is often counterproductive.

My husband and I check our daughter's devices from time to time and have noticed she has multiple accounts on the same social media site. Should we be worried?

It can be a good thing. Many teens have a "real" account and
a "fake" one. The real one is just for their friends—where
they can be themselves without the world seeing. The fake
one is to maintain their public "online" image. The key to
them keeping safe is to ensure that they have a fake name on
their public account and that they don't share any personal
or identifying information. The private account should be
"closed" and their posts visible only to their friends. Regularly
check what they are posting on all their accounts.

> **NADIA:**
> I often look at my daughters' posts, but I step in only if I feel very strongly. Sometimes they've innocently posted something provocative.

Could a predator have asked her to set up the second account as a secret line of contact?

It's unlikely. A predator would probably use a messenger app,
such as WhatsApp or Snapchat, as these are encrypted. If
you are worried, look out for new apps they've installed.

We are planning a big birthday party for my teenager. How can I be sure it doesn't become a shout-out to all the friends of his friends on social media?

KAYE:
When it comes to parties, it's "my house, my rules." Invites go out by text only, and I ask for a guest list so I can check people in at the door. It might not surprise you that we haven't had many teen parties at our house.

There are some true horror stories out there of kids who inadvertently "invited" thousands of people to their parties, which ended in violence, damage, and arrests, so it's no surprise you want to avoid this scenario at all costs. The solution is really very simple: don't use social media to send out invitations. Instead, invite his friends by phone and paper invitations only. If he absolutely must use social media, then be sure the information is shared only with a group of friends he knows and trusts to keep it confidential.

How could an invitation go viral?

The most common ways for this to happen is if your son sets up a public event. If it's not set as a "private" group, anyone on his social media network can potentially see the time, location, and who's going—including anyone who hasn't been invited and perhaps feels left out and total strangers.

Can we stop it once it's out there? What should we do if we can't?

There is really little you can do apart from changing the venue and/or date of the party and locking down the house. Have an adult, or even a security guard, on the premises in case hoards of unknown people show up. You might want to prewarn the police if you are really worried.

PREVENT PARTIES FROM GOING VIRAL

Follow these guidelines to avoid teen party chaos:

• Agree on a guest list and a maximum number of guests (but be prepared for this number to double).

• Agree on some ground rules, such as what time it finishes. Inform the neighbors if the party is at home.

• Ideally, don't use your home so you can avoid things getting damaged. If you can't avoid this, use an outside area.

• Make sure that at least two adults are present, one on the door to check the guest list and one to keep an eye on things.

We've just read a story about how just posting pics of the family barbecue is enough to reveal tons of information. But what are we sharing without realizing it?

When you look closely at a picture, you may see lots of details you might not have considered when you first took it. That landmark in the background shows where you are; a framed photo identifies other family members; a school shirt or team jersey indicates what school your children go to; your car license plate or even an address on a letter on the table can be used to find you. Remember, people can zoom in on images to try to get a better view of these things.

Images can include embedded information about the date, time they were taken, and the type of camera you used. If you have location settings enabled on a camera or app (see pp.90–91), they may even say where they were taken. That's a lot of information to be gleaned, so you need to be careful when you share pictures on social media, and make sure you use your privacy setting to control who can see them—if people can see a photo, they can screenshot or download it.

KAYE:
I have fallen foul of this big time. I posted a video with a quick shot of me opening a letter. Next thing I knew, someone had taken a screenshot and posted my address online. Now I double-check before I upload anything to our page.

But aren't I just sharing the information with friends?

Not necessarily. The 20-plus-page software license agreement nobody reads when they sign up for a photo-sharing or social networking app can include all kinds of surprises as to who can see your images and who they can share them with. As soon as a photo is shared, you potentially lose control over it. A friend might download the photo, send it to somebody else, or upload it to a public website.

The bigger risk, though, is social media. If you're not very careful with your privacy settings, there's a good chance that everything you post is available to everybody on the planet.

1.8 BILLION IMAGES are **UPLOADED** onto social media **EVERY DAY.**

How can I ensure my family shares photos safely?

First, think about where you and your family are posting the photos. Are your account privacy settings turned on? Who's able to see your stuff—friends only, friends of friends, or the entire Internet? Even if it's friends only, have you and your kids been selective in who you connect with, or does your friends' list contain everybody from people who you went to school with to people you met just the once on vacation? Can you trust them all? When were you last in contact with them? Are you even still friends with them?

Second, what is the picture of? Would you be happy to put the photo down on a table in a public coffee shop for other customers and staff to see? Are you happy there's nothing too revealing that a stranger could benefit from by seeing it? This includes anything that may indicate where you live, such as your house number or car license plate, clues to your lifestyle such as items of jewelry and expensive watches, indicators of

PHOTO-SHARING HAZARDS

Think about everything that you could be unintentionally sharing when posting online.

1 Children tagged in photo

2 Car license plate visible

3 Expensive jewelry or other items visible

4 House, house number, road name, and landmarks potentially visible

5 Hashtag that appeals to thieves or online predators

6 Picture liked by a stranger

7 The image is used as the uploader's profile picture, making it visible to everyone on the site (even those who aren't friends)

#kidsinpaddlingpool #summerfun #familytime

where your child goes to school, or anything (such as your children in swimwear) that could appeal to a predator.

Third, are you going to post it as a regular picture on your feed or as a profile picture? If it's a profile picture, most social media sites will set the viewing by default as public, meaning anybody online can see it, whether your other content is public or private. Also, if you tag other friends in a picture, all their friends, who you may not know, will see it, too, if your friends repost it to their page.

What about photos I am in, or my kids are in, that others have taken and/or posted?

While you might guard your photos behind strict security settings, photos of you and your children posted by friends or family members may not be so well protected, and they can be reposted and reposted.

In pretty much every country in the world, having your picture taken is legal, and only in situations where it can be deemed as harassment or a deliberate invasion of privacy do you have legal recourse. So when photos are taken by friends, determine what they're intending to do with them—are they going to post them on their social media or keep them for themselves? There is also the fashion for hashtagging pictures. Are they using tags that could invite trouble—such as #bathtime, #playtime, #kidsonthebeach, and so on that could be searched for by child predators? If you are the slightest bit uncomfortable or unsure, then maybe politely ask your friends not to take the picture with your child in it, or ask them to remove any hashtags you're uncomfortable with.

If it's a social situation, such as a child's birthday party, you could agree to your child being photographed but only if your or your child's name isn't tagged in the picture. If they do, even by accident, you can either ask your friends to remove it later or untag your name yourself. On many social media sites, there are help areas on how to do this.

Fake news is literally making headlines these days. How can I limit my kid's access to the fake stories and false information they see on social media?

You can't shield them from this. They will encounter fake content—news, lifestyle features, photos, and even educational material—through social media and other sites. Many of these stories will be obviously fake, gossipy, or for humor value. However, there are some sites that deliberately set out to generate harmful fake content—such as propaganda, disinformation, and hoaxes—so make sure your kids avoid these once they come to your attention.

How can my child spot a fake story online?

Make sure your child checks the website the story originated from and verifies it with a reputable media outlet (such as CNN or the *New York Times*)—if they are carrying the story, it's likely to be true. Encourage your child to think about whether the site could have an ulterior motive. If it sounds too ridiculous to be true, it probably is.

Is there any problem sharing fake news?

Part of engaging in the social media world is sharing and posting shocking stories found online—"the outrageous is contagious." The problem occurs if your child shares a story that is potentially malicious, rumor-mongering, or libelous against a particular individual or organization. Anything construed as damaging, cruel, or harmful could be seen as a criminal offense. Most social networking sites have terms of acceptable use, so if your child's story violates those, their account could be suspended or they could be banned. If they're sharing with other children or it involves another student, it could be reported to the school or local authorities.

KAYE:
I've been a journalist for 30 years, and I can tell you fake news is often down to nuance and emphasis rather than total lies. I agree that the best antidote is to question stories: Who? What? When? Where? and Why?

NADIA:
My husband and I often watch the news with our girls and talk to them about what we see—including fake news. We have often laughed at some of the most outrageous stories!

TAKEAWAYS

1 BEWARE ONLINE ADDICTION Talk to your child about how "likes" can affect self-esteem. Getting approval online is like getting a mini "high."

2 THINK ABOUT YOUR NETWORK'S REACH Always be mindful that a network of friends includes friends' friends and so on. Know exactly who you are sharing content with.

3 BE SKEPTICAL ABOUT UNKNOWN ONLINE FRIENDS Security settings alone won't protect your kids. Make sure your child is skeptical about a fake friend or stranger and fake content or disinformation.

4 THINK BEFORE POSTING Remember that content is hard to erase. What your child sends out into the digital world is difficult, if not impossible, to retrieve. Photos can be copied and kept forever.

5 DON'T REVEAL TOO MUCH IN PHOTOS Look at your pictures— are there details that could identify you or your location?

6 THINK CAREFULLY ABOUT HASHTAGS Though fun, your pics could be reposted, and seemingly innocent hashtags may mean something risky or dangerous to someone else.

7 KEEP A CHECK ON REALITY Remind your child that not everything they see or read online is true—information can be fake and images enhanced.

8 PROTECT REAL AND FAKE ACCOUNTS Make sure that your child has a "fake" name on their "fake" account and that they never post anything personal on it that could be used by an online predator or blackmailer.

WANT MORE INFO? If this chapter hasn't answered all your questions, try:

CYBERBULLYING AND TROLLS

HOW TO BLOCK AND DISARM ONLINE BULLIES

WHAT YOU NEED TO KNOW

4 IN 5 adolescents have **SEEN HATEFUL COMMENTS** made to **OTHERS**.

KAYE'S EXPERIENCE

You know my biggest fear about cyberbullying?

It's that we don't even know what it is anymore. Once upon a time, you were in no doubt about who the bully was. You knew most of their tricks, you knew where they would be waiting for you, and you'd do your best to take another route and make a beeline for home, to safety.

Nowadays, there is no place of safety. The bully can reach you through the device sitting in your pocket or on your bedside table. You might know who it is; you might not. It might be one person; it might be 20. It might be a kid in your class; it might be a 40-year-old man in another country. There isn't the clear separation of the goodies and the baddies anymore. You can't even be sure that your child isn't, unwittingly or otherwise, another child's bully.

I pushed open my daughter's bedroom door one night to see that she was visibly upset. I gingerly sat on the bed waiting for either an outpouring or a "Leave me alone!" It turned out that she and a bunch of girls she vaguely knew had started to play the Honesty Game in an online group chat, where they all shared their thoughts about each other. You can imagine where that led. Teenage insecurity fueled by physical distance led to some very hurtful "home truths" coming out.

Were they consciously bullying each other? Did my daughter say some stuff she shouldn't have? I'm not sure, but the bottom line is that I had a very distressed child to deal with.

More and more, I am beginning to think that tackling cyberbullies and trolls has less to do with shutting them down and more to do with building your child up—making them more resilient and more aware of what is and isn't acceptable behavior. A friend of mine heads a social media channel that actively recruits young vloggers (video bloggers), and their policy toward trolls and

NADIA:
I couldn't agree more with Kaye on this—our job as parents is to build our children's self-esteem so they can cope with harsh comments.

bullies is to pour pity on them. Instead of allowing them to cast a great, dark, scary shadow over the online world, they squeeze them into a tiny, pathetic little box and stick it in the corner.

Now, don't get me wrong: I am not naive enough to think that a lecture about the cowardly nature of cyberbullies and trolls is going to pacify a weeping child, but it is a message we have to reinforce and a conversation we need to keep having time and time again.

WILL'S EXPERT ANALYSIS

Online bullying can be much more than name-calling. Cyberbullying is when someone repeatedly threatens, harasses, mocks, or abuses someone online or via text messaging or apps, often over more than one online session. Trolling is when someone makes a comment online to upset someone else for their own or their friends' amusement. The lines between the two are blurry, and both can involve hate crime, driven by prejudice toward, for instance, a person's race or sexuality. Cyberbullying and trolling are a daily reality for many. We can't stop bullies, but we can control them. The key is to know how to limit them.

The appeal of online bullying and trolling is that it can be done anonymously. Perpetrators don't have to face their victims and may believe that they can pick on others without suffering any

25%
of children have
**RECEIVED HATEFUL
COMMENTS**
online.

WILL'S CASE STUDY

PREDATORS FLOCK TO SOCIAL MEDIA PAGE OF CYBERBULLIED BOY

I dealt with a case where a client discovered that his son was posting porn online, as well as writing abusive posts about teachers and students. The first my client knew about it was when the school called—other parents had complained. It turned out that the boy's phone password was stolen by another child who was "shoulder surfing" (watching over his shoulder) as he opened his phone. When the boy was at field day, the other child broke into his locker, found his phone, turned off his social media privacy settings, and then used the boy's page to share the pornography and abuse.

consequences themselves. Prepare your child for the fact that there are bullies online and that your child may encounter them at some point. Talk to them about how to deal with this.

How big is the problem?

Cyberbullying can happen at any age, but it's particularly prevalent in the 12–17 age group. Boys are more often subjected to abuse when playing video games, and girls are more likely to be bullied about their appearance or popularity via text or on social media.

Sadly, children from ethnic minorities and those with disabilities are most likely to be targeted, with 24 percent of children aged 13–18 years old being singled out because of their gender, sexual orientation, race, religion, or disability. If you or your child are from any kind of minority group, then bullying and trolling may also focus on things specific to that minority, such as physical stereotypes, traditional clothing, gender identity, and so on.

In cases of bullying among peers, cyberbullying often happens on smartphones and can take the form of sustained abusive text messages, videos, or memes. It also happens in comments boards, virtual chat rooms, and on apps where the offender can't be seen.

How can it affect your family?

Nobody wants their child to be bullied, and online bullying is particularly hard to deal with: the bullies can be anonymous or disappear, and it can happen around the clock, not just at school.

Bullying often targets insecurities and can have a devastating effect on (already shaky) self-confidence. As a result, your child's behavior may change: they may become anxious or depressed, or even self-harm. One sign to watch for is a sudden interest in their intellect or appearance, with questions such as "Am I clever?" or "Have I got weird hair?"

How do you prevent it from affecting your family?

Your child needs to understand that there are stupid, silly, and sad people who take pleasure in getting a reaction out of people by upsetting them, and if your child posts anywhere publicly, they may encounter trolls. These trolls can be avoided by sticking to social media sites you can control—for example, a social network with good privacy settings can prevent trolls' messages from getting through, make them easy to block, or allow you to disable comments.

Tell your child to let you know if they've experienced abuse online and that you're there to support and help, not judge, them.

What should you do if it's already happened?

The golden rule: don't feed the trolls. The more your child reacts and the more upset they are, the more fun the troll is having. Say nothing and their fun stops. If your child keeps being trolled when they go on a particular site, game, or app, find out if it's always the same person. If so, report them to the site administrators or block them (see p.37) if the service or app allows. If it keeps recurring, keep reporting the person. If you can't block them, use a new site (though your child may argue that they have to use that site because their friends do), or create a new profile. Parents of younger children can research sites in advance to check which ones are most secure.

Insults and threats in videos, texts, or tweets can easily happen via cell phone. Don't retaliate or reply. Keep a record of all the calls. If you know who it is (or if their number hasn't been withheld), contact the school (if it's another student) or give the information to the police who will generate a crime reference number. Pass this to the cell phone service provider with times and dates of calls to help them trace the caller. Then to avoid any further contact, get a new SIM card and replace the number.

When should you seek outside help?

Ongoing, repeated, and persistent harassment is illegal. Examples of criminal harassment include repeatedly saying things such as, "You're stupid" or "ugly," "I want to hurt or kill you," or "I want to hurt or kill somebody you know." It may also include using offensive emojis or posting offensive images or videos. If your child is being persistently harassed across multiple sites and apps by the same people, call the police. Ask your child the questions in the panel (see right) and document any evidence (see pp.226–227).

> **KAYE:**
> I often worry that, in trying to work out if one of my girls is being bullied, I end up interrogating her. I find it's best to ask about it in stages with general questions about how things are going.

QUESTIONS TO ASK YOUR CHILD

If your child is being bullied online, gently ask these questions, avoiding an interrogation. This will help give you a full picture of the situation.

- Who is upsetting you?
- When did it start?
- Where did it start?
- What are they saying?
- When are they doing it?
- Why do you think they are saying that?

PARENTS' QUESTIONS ANSWERED

I'm worried that my daughter is friends with some "mean girls" on social media.

**1 IN 8
YOUNG PEOPLE
have been
BULLIED on
SOCIAL MEDIA.**

Every community has cliques, such as the mean girls at school or the queen bees of the PTA: they're the groups some people want to join, the special clubs where not everybody is welcome. And sometimes those groups are actively unpleasant to others. It's not unique to children: there are plenty of adult groups who are happy to gossip maliciously and gang up on other people. You likely won't stop your daughter from wanting to be part of the group, but you can explain to her that if the group does anything to hurt anybody else, such as constantly picking on and victimizing somebody, they could all end up—your daughter included—in serious trouble. A lot of the children who "pile on" others on social media don't realize that they could actually be committing a criminal offense. Your daughter might not appreciate the emotional damage she and her friends could be doing, either: there have been many cases of children who have self-harmed or even killed themselves after being relentlessly bullied.

Can she unfriend them, and won't they know?
That depends on the site or app. On Facebook, you can unfollow someone so that you're still their Facebook friend but no longer see their posts. However, many social media sites and apps are binary: you're either connected or you

aren't. One of the best ways to leave a group discreetly and without anybody noticing is to take a lower profile: reading less often, posting fewer things, leaving fewer likes, and taking longer to reply to messages.

If your daughter does unfriend the group and they find out and confront her, she could use an excuse, such as the site had a glitch (Twitter, for example, has had problems, with connections suddenly disappearing for no reason); the site kicked her off for no reason; or "my parents took away my phone." Lying isn't ideal but could help your child to feel less stressed in this type of situation and prevent a confrontation.

NADIA:
This is definitely a useful tactic. I do sometimes tell my girls to use me as a foil if they are finding it difficult to get out of awkward situations.

What can I do if the group's sending abusive messages or threats or spreading rumors?

If she's part of the group, she's complicit. I believe every responsible parent should have a zero-tolerance approach to any kind of bullying—make it clear that if it happens, you'll confiscate her device and shut down her access to the Internet. If the behavior is more serious, such as threatening physical harm, your daughter needs to understand that this is a criminal offense and that the police could get involved. Getting a criminal record could affect her life long after she's forgotten the other girls' names.

My mixed-race son is receiving a lot of racist comments about his hair and skin color from what looks like a hate group. Is it?

It could be, or it could simply be other children. Children can be cruel and pick on any difference they find. Your son might be used to the odd stupid comment—which is not acceptable—

but this sounds more persistent and definitely should not be tolerated. To victimize anyone for their race or racial traits, such as their hair or skin color, is a "hate incident," which is illegal and unacceptable regardless of the child's age.

So far it's "just words," but can't words themselves be inciting hatred, and isn't that a crime?

If it's just words, this is usually categorized as a hate incident as opposed to a hate crime. It's still serious, but many law enforcement agencies will judge the severity based on the age of the perpetrators. If they're children, the police may not be able to do a great deal. If they simply don't understand the gravity of their words, a single warning might suffice, informing them that what they're doing is illegal. If they're adults, more serious action needs to be taken by the police.

How can I identify who it is?

On a social media platform, contact the site administrators, who may be able to identify who is sending the racist comments, for example, from their IP address or username. If it's serious, the site can contact the police who can use additional tools to trace them.

Surely they are in violation of the terms of use on the site—how do we shut them down?

If threats are on a website or on multiple sites, you can contact the "report abuse" sections on these sites and tell them what has been happening. Each social media site has "acceptable terms of use," and the administrators can block the perpetrator or suspend or cancel their account and remove their posts. It can be more challenging in places such as the United States, though, where people can use the First Amendment rights to free speech as a cloak for hate speech, whereas in Europe most hate speech has been criminalized. Alternatively, your child can change his profile picture or username or steer clear of the site altogether and delete his account.

25%
of children have **WITNESSED RACIST** or **HATE MESSAGES** online.

If abuse has taken place via email or text, take screenshots and record dates, times, locations, and usernames. If the perpetrator is from your child's school, contact the school first, or even their parents; otherwise, inform the police.

12%
of young people have **ADMITTED TO BULLYING SOMEONE ELSE** online.

> **I'm horrified: I've been told by another parent that my son, along with some friends, is bullying another boy online. What should I do?**

It is a good idea to confiscate his device(s) first of all to ensure that he can't continue what he was doing. It may seem drastic, but you have to stop any action that could be interpreted as bullying immediately.

Find out the reasons your son is doing this—what he thought he was doing and why. Sometimes kids do things without thinking them through, so try to get him to see how his behavior might affect others and how he would feel if the tables were turned.

If you are getting nowhere with the conversation, or if he doesn't seem remorseful—genuinely remorseful, not just mumbling "sorry" without making eye contact—you may need to seek professional help for him, such as counseling.

You may want to reach out to the victim or the victim's family, but I would recommend avoiding this because it could make the situation worse, especially if you're not sure of your child's actions. The best person to apologize is your son.

KAYE:
When talking to your son, it might be best to avoid the word "bullying" at first. Instead, ask questions such as "Could that make someone feel bad?" It's important that he makes the link between his words and the impact those words could have on others.

Can he be traced by the police or other authorities?
Unless your child is some kind of technological whiz kid with the kind of hacking skills you only see in the movies, the answer is almost certainly yes—online bullies are rarely

master criminals who escape detection. Almost everything we do electronically leaves a trace somewhere, and that trace is often enough to identify the person who posted or sent the email or text message. And, of course, the victims of bullying or harassment have probably kept copies of everything.

What are the possible consequences?

That depends on his age. The age of criminal responsibility differs from state to state, but it's usually around 10–12 years old; once you've reached that age, you can be prosecuted for criminal behavior. And as we've already discovered, online bullying is often criminal behavior: that could mean a criminal record and, if the bullying has been really bad and its impact severe, time in a juvenile prison.

My daughter is on Instagram. The thing is, it's not her. She has no idea who's behind it. What's going on?

There are several possible scenarios. It might be a joke account set up by a friend of your daughter, or it might be a malicious account set up by a cyberstalker, cyberbully, or someone your daughter knows, with the aim of damaging her reputation. Someone may have gained access to your daughter's original account, or it could be a duplicate account created by an agency to bolster likes on their clients' pages. Fake accounts are common on most social media sites.

Okay, so how do I know for sure if it's a joke account?

Take a look at the page and see if you can work out the motivation behind it. Does it look like a joke of some sort? If so, then it's probably a friend who thinks they're being funny. Tell your daughter not to mention it to any of her friends: whoever's behind it is desperate for it to be noticed, so if they don't get a reaction, they'll often give the game away by mentioning it themselves.

Before you report it to Instagram, it's worth asking the creator (if you know who they are) to take it down. How would they feel if someone did a fake profile about them?

How do we find out who created it if we don't know?

If you don't know who it is, report it to Instagram's administrators immediately and ask the site's administrators to remove it. Instagram acts fairly quickly when it's told about a problem. If your child is under 13 years old (this is the minimum age for an Instagram account), they'll shut the account down right away.

However, the administrators probably won't tell you who set up the account, because that information isn't given to other users, which makes sense: you wouldn't want Instagram to tell someone else your daughter's personal details simply because that person asked for them.

If it's a duplicate, can't Instagram just stop people from creating fake accounts?

Instagram does try to stop people setting these up, but the site admins can't even keep up with all the fake celebrity profiles, let alone those of everybody else. Once users report fakes, Instagram is usually pretty quick to take them down.

What if the account used to be her normal account but someone else has taken it over?

Someone could be hijacking your daughter's identity, maybe to humiliate or embarrass her by controlling her content and distorting the message her account sends. If this is the case, then check whether she can still log in with her existing password. If she can, then chances are it's a "drive-by

In November 2017, there were

270

MILLION FAKE ACCOUNTS on **FACEBOOK**. That number is **INCREASING**.

50% of **PEOPLE** in the US have been **VICTIMS** of **HACKING**.

hack"—which means she's left her device sitting somewhere unlocked and somebody took the opportunity to mess with her Instagram, or she has been "phished" (see p.162). If this happened, change her password, review her security settings, and then monitor activity on her account. Setting up two-factor authentication (see p.205) can help prevent this from happening again in the future.

If she can't get in, things are more serious. First of all, she'll need to contact Instagram to get a new password; then, she'll need to make sure her password hasn't been changed on any other sites. If it has, she will need to contact the site administrators on those sites, too.

Does this mean all her online personal information is compromised?

Not necessarily, but if she used the same password on any other website or service, she needs to change those passwords immediately. Set up two-factor authentication on these accounts, too, if possible (it is on all of the big-name services).

The most important thing to think about is her email. If somebody has access to her email inbox, they could change the password on any of her social media accounts. That person just has to click the "forgotten password" option on the site, and your daughter will be sent a reset password link to her email address. The hacker can log in to her email with the stolen password and use the link to change the password of that social media account, locking your daughter out.

I can't stress this enough: if you have any reason to think someone else may know any of your daughter's passwords, change all of them immediately. Never use the same password on more than one site or service.

Can they pretend to be her and blame her for things they've done? Can they now access all her images?

Yes, and possibly—if they've got access to the account, they've got access to anything that's been posted to it. You have to be careful with anything you post online, since it's really easy to grab photos from social media and misuse them. There's lots of software out there, such as Deepfake, that can scan selfies people have shared publicly on services such as Instagram and make fake pornographic videos from them. Deepfake isn't a huge problem, or at least it isn't just yet. The bigger worry here is identity theft. It's possible for a compromised account to be used as part of a whole faked or stolen identity.

There's a small risk of reputational damage from a compromised account, with people thinking what's posted or shared from it was posted or shared by your daughter. That means it's important to act quickly when you're reporting an account issue—the sooner Instagram knows about it, the sooner the problem can be stopped. If you're worried about reputational damage, you can post elsewhere to alert people that somebody's faking your daughter's Instagram posts.

KAYE:
Will, this is horrendous. Is there anything our kids can do to protect themselves from this?

WILL:
There are two things you can do that may help. First, post low-resolution images so that other people get only blurred images when they try to download them. Second, tell them to put a faint watermark over their face in images (search online for instructions on how to do this).

My daughter is a beauty blogger, and it makes me worry about the abuse girls get online and all the haters out there. She's considering vlogging. Is there anything specifically you can do about trolls on YouTube?

First, take a deep breath and be prepared. Anything your child posts could create a reaction—good or bad.

I've worked with many female celebrities who've experienced really vicious trolling. They can either learn to ignore the comments, disable the comments, or stay off social media altogether. The same applies to any kind of public figure, such as a vlogger. Certainly, for younger children, I'd advise disabling the comments feature initially. You can do this in the settings page of her channel by selecting the "video

NADIA:
My daughters both want to set up YouTube channels, but I've said no because of the vicious comments. I have enough trouble dealing with those sorts of comments at my age!

KAYE:
I find my kids are actually more robust when it comes to strangers' abusive comments. It's the ones from friends and people who they know that really affect them.

50%
of victims of **BULLYING** said the hurtful **COMMENTS** related to their **APPEARANCE.**

manager" or Channel Settings option then manage comment settings on individual videos.

For older children, comments can be part of the fun, which means they'll almost certainly be trolled. As the saying goes, "haters gonna hate." Sadly, it's just a fact that some people on the Internet are awful, and, if you allow comments, those people will comment on your public posts and videos. If your daughter wants to blog online, she needs to be prepared for it.

Why is there such an emphasis on her looks, her skin, and her weight? It gets really personal.

Beauty blogging is all about physical appearance, so of course people focus on that. Some people are driven by their own insecurities about their looks or weight so make themselves feel better by picking on others. It's not much consolation, but remind yourself that anybody being unpleasant to your daughter is probably not terribly happy themselves.

Should she just ignore negative comments and insults or respond? How can she disarm the troll?

Remember, don't feed the trolls! Your daughter might come up with a witty, clever, pithy response, the kind of thing people will quote admiringly for centuries to come, but it's generally a waste of time. The troll wants a reaction, and, for them, any reaction is a good reaction. The troll wants to know that they've upset her or got under her skin. If she replies, she's letting them know they have. If your daughter doesn't reply, sooner or later they'll go and find another blogger to troll. It's not uncommon for trolls to pester lots of different people online. Explain it's more about the troll than her.

Is the best action to shut down her blog or vlog?

That's really up to her. Talk to her. Does the joy of blogging or vlogging more than compensate for the hassle of the trolls? If it reaches the point where the trolls have taken all the fun out of it, then it's a good idea to disable the comments so she can carry on vlogging without having to deal with trolls. But if she's okay despite the trolling, it might actually be good in the long run: she's demonstrating the resilience that we all need to develop when we're growing up and learning to deal with the adult world.

NADIA:
In our house, we use the mantra "Those who mind don't matter, and those who matter don't mind!" It gives me a real buzz to hear my daughters quoting it to friends in need.

TAKEAWAYS

1 DON'T FEED THE TROLLS Disable comments, block cyberbullies, and never reply to negativity.

2 WATCH FOR BEHAVIORAL SIGNS New insecurities, low self-esteem, and social withdrawal can all be indicators that your child is being victimized online.

3 CHECK CHAT ROOM MESSAGES AND TEXTS Cyberbullying usually happens via the written word—where the bully or troll can't be seen.

4 REPORT PERSISTENT HARASSMENT Block harassers or report them to the site admins. Bullying and hate crime shouldn't be tolerated.

5 BEWARE OF OPPORTUNITY HACKS A social media page can be sabotaged if your child leaves their device lying around unlocked.

6 PROTECT YOUR PICTURES Consider uploading smaller images to protect against people stealing them.

WANT MORE INFO? If this doesn't answer all your questions, try:

- Cyberstalking and Tracking, pp.85–87
- Catfishing, pp.99–100
- Coercion, Extortion, and Blackmail, pp.137–139

CYBERSTALKING AND TRACKING

HOW TO KEEP YOUR KIDS' LOCATIONS PRIVATE

WHAT YOU NEED TO KNOW

KAYE'S PERSPECTIVE

It was a spooky moment. I was at home in beautiful Scotland when Nadia called and asked where my eldest daughter was. I said she was away with friends, unsure of the exact address. "Well, I know where she is," said Nadia and reeled off an address that sounded vaguely right. I thought she was going a bit bonkers, but when I checked, she was bang on; she knew exactly where Charly was. And I didn't. That's when I learned about Snap Map, an addition to Snapchat. Nadia's daughter Maddie had located Charly to show Nadia how it works.

We were flabbergasted. It gave an exact, real-time location and even showed who she was with and if the other people were also Snapchat friends. The possibilities for misuse started to run through our heads: a jealous boyfriend, a left-out friend, an older individual trying to stalk them. We put a video on our social media channel expressing our concern and got more than 30 million hits.

Snapchat got in touch with us, and we met with a senior executive who tried to reassure us that only "friends" had access to the information and only then if the user was not in "ghost mode." If you select ghost mode, you remain under cover. When we asked whether these features had been tested on the teenage brain, the executive from Snapchat admitted they had not. Yes, you can put it in ghost mode, but you have to want to. And, yes, you are visible only to friends, but the app allows you to have up to 2,500 "friends," and, as we all know, the more "friends" you have, the more popular you are. In teen world, popularity is everything. (You can now select which Snapchat friends can see your location.)

Snapchat isn't the only platform that offers a "finding service." The reality is that, if you have a smartphone, you can probably be tracked. It might start out as a bad joke, a crush, or an infatuation, but the potential is there for it to turn into something sinister.

There were an estimated

2.5M

CYBERSTALKING CASES in the US between 2014 and 2017.

WILL'S EXPERT ANALYSIS

Cyberstalking is where harassment and trolling advance into something more direct, more systematic, and more persistent. Cyberstalkers "follow" victims across multiple digital or online platforms, such as email, chat rooms, social media, or text, building a web to home in on their victims, maybe sharing personal information online or blackmailing them. They may track a victim's movements by checking locations in social media posts. The stalker may be a stranger or known to the victim, and though this type of obsessive harassment is relatively unusual, it can cause huge distress.

Cyberstalkers may be motivated by paranoia, a desire for a romantic association, or retribution or have a delusional fixation. For example, the stalker may have misconstrued a conversation or seen a picture of the victim that creates an obsessive love disorder.

A cyberstalker isn't always the clichéd "weirdo" with little contact with the outside world; I've dealt with several cases where a stalker was, on the surface, perfectly normal.

KAYE:
Will, at what point do you know you're being cyberstalked rather than simply getting unwelcome attention? You may not realize it's the same person creating multiple accounts.

WILL:
It becomes cyberstalking when the same user messages more regularly, every time you go online, and/or on multiple sites or apps.

How big is the problem?

Statistics on the number of cyberstalking cases are variable and at best can only be estimated, since many cases go unreported or even undetected. However, one major Internet service provider said that

OVERFRIENDLY WAITER AT VACATION RESORT STALKS YOUNG GIRL AND HER FAMILY

I had a case where a client's daughter was cyberstalked on vacation. One of the waiters was extremely charming and helpful, and he'd often give the daughter treats such as extra ice cream. At first, it seemed perfectly normal and good fun; however, things started to get strange. The family would go out to dinner, and, after a while, the waiter would turn up in his regular clothes. It was happening so often that the parents became concerned. They realized what was going on only when their daughter said that the waiter was following her on Instagram. When she posted a picture, he identified where she was from the background.

AVOID BROADCASTING your child's day-to-day routines by **POSTING** about **PLACES THEY REGULARLY VISIT.**

it dealt with regular cases of cyberstalking each month throughout 2017, compared with almost no cases being reported during the whole of 2015 and 2016.

Statistically, women and girls are more likely to be stalked than men or boys, and stalkers are most likely to be male. The main hunting grounds for cyberstalkers are the big social media sites. That may be because many children don't use privacy settings on social media or because most teens don't report worrying online behavior, either because they're unaware of what to look out for or because they are worried about a real-life confrontation.

How can it affect your family?

While cyberbullying and trolling generally remain limited to one site or chat room, cyberstalking intrudes on the life of the victim and those around them. The perpetrators track their victims across the Internet to gain as much information about them as possible.

If you introduce stricter privacy settings to your child's social media accounts, then the stalker might stalk friends and family for information to indicate what your child is doing, saying, or feeling and who they are with. Accounts may be contacted to gain information or hacked so the stalker can post offensive content on your child's page that appears to come from friends and family.

How do you prevent it from happening?

Make a cyberstalker's life as difficult as possible. Make sure that your kids' posts and friend lists aren't public (check their privacy settings on the site) and that the rest of the family's aren't, either.

Your child should never give away their location by posting about it or by keeping their phone's location sharing setting turned on (see p.207). We all have routines, and children even more so. It's frighteningly easy to build a picture of someone's daily movements when they are always posting or sharing their location.

It's also important to maintain an open dialogue with your child so that they are comfortable telling you if anything worries them, such as contact (or repeated contact) from a stranger. The earlier you know about a problem, the more easily it can be dealt with.

KAYE:
I want to protect my kids, but I don't want them to be paranoid wrecks. Should I really be telling them they can't post a picture of them and their friends at a concert on the outside chance they might be stalked?

WILL:
Nobody wants their child to be paranoid, but they do want them to be careful. Just tell them not to post everything they do and everywhere they go day to day. One-off events should be fine.

What should you do if it's already happened?

First, create a list of online locations where the cyberstalker has appeared, and take screenshots of what they've been doing. This gives you an idea of how many sites they are using and which ones you need to check your child's privacy settings on. It also helps the authorities to identify the perpetrator if you don't know who it is.

Contact the departments that deal with online abuse on the sites (if they have them—the big social networks all do) to ask for the stalker's account to be blocked or, if you have enough evidence, terminated. Be aware that they may return with a new account, so you'll need to report that, too, if this is the case.

Now visit your child's profile pages and review what they're sharing. What can you see? Change your child's privacy settings to ensure that they are hiding anything you don't want to be shared. Make sure, too, that your child has two-factor authentication (see p.205) set up for every social media account—so any account detail changes must be confirmed on a separate device, preventing their passwords from being hacked and changed without them knowing.

Finally, warn friends and family that your child is being targeted in case the cyberstalker turns their attention toward them.

When should you seek outside help?

If, despite your efforts, the problem gets worse—the stalker makes more frequent contact, sends malicious messages or material, creates fake social media accounts, and/or approaches friends or family—it's probably criminal behavior, and if you haven't already contacted the police, you should do so now. In many cases, site administrators won't do anything unless the police are also involved.

Unfortunately, the next step is to change your child's routine. Randomize the times that your child is allowed to log on to social media, making sure that they aren't online at their usual times. If the harassment has been particularly worrying, suggest that your child takes a complete online break until the police have concluded their investigation. It's important that the break isn't so long that your child becomes scared to go online at all. Try chaperoning your child online if you both agree, or reassure them that you're close at hand.

> **NADIA:**
> This is a good point, Will. As parents, we have a tricky job making children aware of the dangers without making them too anxious to go online at all.

GIVING AWAY THEIR LOCATION?

The ways in which your child's location could be made public are:

- Your child posting about their location directly

- Your child hashtagging their location in their posts

- Your child's photo apps and social media accounts having geotagging enabled

- Friends and family tagging your child or posting about them being in certain locations

- An online friend sharing or retweeting your child's post to a wider audience

PARENTS' QUESTIONS ANSWERED

> **There's this really creepy guy who keeps following my daughter on social media. She blocks and reports him, but then he's back almost immediately with a new account. What can she do?**

What starts as harassment can develop into cyberstalking; either way, it's not nice. Your daughter needs to tell him that if he doesn't leave her alone, she'll report him. Take a photo or screenshot of his various comments and your warning along with the date and time, so you can track how long the problem continues if the warning doesn't scare him off. Don't respond to any of his messages after the warning is sent.

How does he keep changing his identity, and what can we do about it?

That depends on the site, but it's very easy to create a new online profile—generally all you need is an email address the site doesn't already have a profile registered to. There are lots of free email services, and most have no identity checks.

If someone is using multiple identities, keep a note of and report all of them. Look for clues that it's the same person, such as familiar patterns of speech. Again, it's vital that your daughter doesn't reply or react—this "feeds" the stalker. Take written notes and screenshots of any messages he sends.

Is there any software that can filter him out?

That depends on the site; for example, on some social networks, you can block specific people, or even specific words. Check the site or service's "Help" section. It will often provide a dedicated guide on what it considers online abuse, how to deal with problematic behavior or people, and even how to help others do so.

What evidence do we need to report him to the social media site or the police?

The more detailed your evidence, the better (see pp.226–227). Record what the stalker says or sends, as well as the date, time, and username. Keep screenshots of their comments since online posts can often be deleted or changed by the person who sent them. It's also worth keeping a list of links to posts that the stalker has commented on. Send everything to the site admins.

She's worried he might turn up in real life and confront her if we take this to the police. What can we do to prevent him from doing this?

Reassure her that she has done the right thing in telling you and that the problem is easier to sort out while it's an online issue only. Gathering online evidence can help to identify and stop the stalker if he starts to follow her in the real world.

Encourage your daughter to avoid using or posting on the social media sites that she is being stalked on. If the messages are via text, consider getting her a new phone number—most networks will allow you to do this for a small fee. This will help prevent the stalker from making contact with her (make sure that she doesn't post the new number on social media and only gives it to trusted friends). Finally, make especially sure that neither she nor her friends post their whereabouts online and that she's managed the location sharing settings on each app to disable location tracking (see p.207).

If you are really concerned, change aspects of your daughter's routine where possible. Encounters that appear to be spontaneous often aren't. The stalker may have been tracking your daughter's activities through her online posts for a while. Changing her routine can make it more difficult for him to predict her whereabouts.

43%
of cyberstalking victims in the US felt they needed to **CHANGE THEIR CONTACT DETAILS** as a result of being stalked.

> **We were horrified when we discovered we could track our kids down to a few yards using smartphone apps. Surely, if we can track our kids, other people can, too?**

Yes, all smartphones have tracking technology that is built into their means of connecting to the Internet (for example, GPRS, 2G, 3G, 4G, and Wi-Fi). This technology is essential for searching the web, receiving emails and messages, and using maps. Most apps have location features so they can provide helpful services, such as giving you the right directions, informing you on which restaurants or gas stations are nearby, or letting you know the showtimes for the nearest movie theaters. This technology is accurate to within a few yards and can be incredibly helpful.

ICLOUD TRACKING

gives away your location. The "Find My iPhone" app means that **ANYONE WHO CAN ACCESS YOUR APPLE ID** account can **TRACK YOUR PHONE'S LOCATION.**

FIND MY KIDS

Location sharing apps can be a useful tool for parents to find out where their kids are. However, children need to make sure that they and their friends are revealing their location only to people who can be trusted.

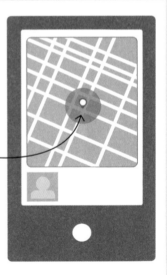

Apps, such as Apple's Find My iPhone, allow parents to keep track of their children by showing the location of their children's devices on a map.

And that's fine: it's what makes smartphones so useful. The problem comes when we share location information without realizing it, or without realizing what other people can do with it. For example, at one point, Snapchat enabled you to search for primary schools in an area (this is no longer the case). Features that seem really handy in a software company's "ideas" meeting aren't so handy in a world of stalkers and other villains.

On phones and tablets, apps that want to use location information usually have to ask for the user's permission. Apple devices are particularly good at this: if an app wants location data, it not only has to ask your permission, but it also has to convince Apple's moderators that it needs that data in the first place. However, apps that have already been installed can be sneaky. For example, an app that didn't ask for location data last month may now use it in the version 3.2.1 update, and it might ask for this as part of the revised terms and conditions that very few of us ever bother to read—we simply scroll down and press "Accept." Social media apps are particularly notorious for requesting ever more data from us; they want to have as much information as possible, often to improve app performance or new features.

I personally believe that children should have their location services disabled on everything except emergency or safety features or apps that help them—for example, taxi or ride-sharing apps to get them home safely or speedily or maps that can provide directions in case they get lost.

How can I get my children to protect themselves but still use apps? What are sensible location sharing checks?

Location services aren't just on or off; there's also a "only when I'm using the app" option. That's the best one. Where apps can share your child's location with others, such as on Snapchat, make sure only people they really know can access that location information.

PROTECT YOUR CHILD by setting location sharing to "ONLY WHEN USING THE APP." This prevents closed apps from sharing your child's location.

Can my kids be tracked through their friends' posts or tagged photos, even if they don't post or reveal the location themselves?

Yes, you can have the most privacy-protected phone in the world, but if one of your child's friends posts online that they're both at the local Chinese takeout or uploads a photo that your child is tagged in, then people will know where they are. There's very little you or your child can do about this other than warning others of the risks and asking friends not to tag you or your child on social media. Some sites, such as Facebook, let you know when someone has posted a picture of you so you can untag yourself.

NADIA:
I was horrified recently when I saw some of Maddie's friends were posting their exact location on Instagram. It was something we hadn't even considered.

Are there any known stalker apps or surveillance software that I need to be aware of?

Yes, although not "legitimate" ones on iPhones or iPads—Apple specifically bans apps in their App Store that spy on other people without their express permission. You can still be tracked via Find My Phone or Find My Friends if you don't specifically limit or disable those features, or if someone finds out the username and password to your Apple ID.

Surveillance and tracking is more of an issue on Android, which doesn't have the same level of restrictions on what can be installed on a device. It is also possible to "jailbreak" any smartphone (including iPhones). This is the term used when the operating software that is installed on the smartphone is deliberately altered to remove restrictions that were imposed by the manufacturer, and it allows users to install unregistered or illegal apps (including spyware).

Some attacks allow hackers remote access to a device through phishing (see p.162). However, a cyberstalker will generally need physical access to your child's phone as well as a Wi-Fi connection in order to load or install spyware onto your child's device. The golden rules to avoid this scenario are to have two-factor authentication set up, which requires a second password to infiltrate an account (see p.205), and a strong device PIN number; to tell your child to never leave their devices sitting around unlocked; and to always have at least one backup copy of anything important. There's more information about setting up devices on pp.202–217.

How would I know if a spyware app had been installed on my kids' device?

It's probably unlikely that you will be able to find the apps on your kids' phones. Unfortunately, they're not always easy to spot, and they're often specifically designed that way for obvious reasons. That's why it's so important to prevent stalker apps from getting onto a device in the first place. However, there are some red flags to look out for:

- The home page of your child's browser goes to an unusual website without their consent.
- Your child's default search page changes search engine (e.g., from Google to something else).
- Your child gets system notifications or pop-ups with unusual messages.
- Your child can see extra icons for systems at the top right or bottom right of your screen (near the symbol indicating your signal strength).
- Your child finds extra bookmarks or shortcuts that they haven't saved on their desktop.

How do I disable stalker apps or surveillance software if they are installed?

If you suspect that there is spyware on your child's device, take a quick look through their apps. I would recommend you try to keep a note of all the apps installed on your child's device as a general habit anyway, as this not only makes sure that you can detect anything unusual quickly, but it also keeps you easily informed as to which ones your child is using regularly. Are there any apps your child doesn't recognize or know (see p.203 and p.215)? If there are and the device is an Apple or Android phone or tablet, you can simply delete the

KEEP DEVICES SAFE AT ALL TIMES so a stalker can't install spyware: make sure your kids don't leave their phones **LYING AROUND UNLOCKED.**

suspicious apps. If you find any suspicious apps, I would also recommend changing the passwords to all of your child's online accounts (such as their email, messenger apps, and social media). Do this on a different device. Only log back into these accounts on your child's device once the suspicious apps have been removed.

If you can't find any strange apps but are still suspicious, the phone may have been "jailbroken" or "rooted." You can reverse the jailbreak by resetting the device (see p.209). This should remove any spyware.

If your child has a laptop, run a system scan with the antivirus and antimalware software installed on the device to detect and remove any spyware. If you don't have security software installed, search online for legitimate "spyware removal software," install it, and use this to remove the problem files (see p.209).

TAKEAWAYS

1 ENSURE THAT YOUR CHILD'S POSTS AREN'T PUBLIC
Cyberstalkers are resourceful, so check privacy settings. If you think your child is being stalked, ask family and friends to check their settings, too.

2 SET UP STRONG PRIVACY SETTINGS The stronger your child's settings, the harder your child is to find.

3 DON'T REVEAL ROUTINES Avoid regular posts that give away a child's daily movements.

4 ...OR LOCATIONS Set the location sharing setting for Photos and other apps to "off" or to "only when using the app."

5 KEEP A RECORD If you suspect your child is being stalked, get them to screenshot all suspicious messages and comments.

6 REPORT STALKERS Pass on your suspicions to social media sites, and if you're particularly concerned, contact the police. Don't delete any of the evidence from the device

7 NEVER LEAVE DEVICES UNMANNED If you think spyware has been installed, back up information then restore the device to factory settings.

8 KNOW YOUR APPS Keep a note of what apps your child has on their device and make sure that they delete any that they don't use.

9 USE 2FA Make sure that all accounts and apps have 2FA set up where possible (see p.205).

10 BETTER SAFE If someone seems to know too much about your child or your child's device is acting strangely, reset the device.

WANT MORE INFO? If this doesn't answer all your questions, try:

GROOMING

PROTECTING YOUR CHILD
FROM ONLINE PREDATORS

WHAT YOU NEED TO KNOW

NADIA'S EXPERIENCE

You won't believe this, but I am actually worried about the fact that I don't worry enough about online grooming! That's motherhood for you! Let me explain.

Given that Mark and I are very open, "switched on" (cringe, I know) parents and given that we are always up for talking about anything bothering our girls at any time of night or day, we assume that our girls would never fall prey to an online groomer.

"After all," we say to ourselves, "isn't it only children that are isolated, unloved, ignored, or uncared for that are vulnerable?" Surely it couldn't happen to our kids because we've had "the talk." We've carefully and compassionately laid out (in no uncertain terms) that there are, at best, hapless souls out there prepared to do anything to "get" a girlfriend and, at worst, ruthless pedophiles on the prowl hiding behind avatars. We've described the red flags to watch out for. So we've done good, right? They know it would be crazy to start up a conversation with someone online that they didn't know in person... don't they?

And this is where the worry really starts to kick in—what if our girls actually think that we are hysterical drama queens? What if they've merely nodded in agreement to shut us up so they can get back upstairs to chat to a load of weirdos masquerading as kids their age? How would we ever know? After all, being a teenager is ALL about having secrets and breaking the rules. What if the only rule they feel they can break with us is to go rogue on social media? This worry overwhelms me and Mark.

If I ever ask who they're talking to, should I always believe whatever they say? How do I know they're telling the truth? And this is where it all becomes utterly terrifying to be a parent in the era of smartphones. Oh dear! I've got myself in a right pickle!

"Maddddieeee …. Kikiiiiii … come downstairs now!"

7 YEARS is the average length of time children take to **REPORT A FIRST INCIDENT OF ABUSE**. Many said **SOMEONE SPOTTING THE SIGNS** would have helped.

WILL'S EXPERT ANALYSIS

Grooming is the gradual, subtle, and harmful manipulation of a vulnerable person, usually a child, as illustrated in the case below. It's what sexual predators, cults, and even terrorists do: they gradually gain their victims' trust so that they can exploit them, often sexually. In the security field, we sometimes call it "human hacking," or "social engineering."

Groomers are often very intelligent people who use a wide range of tactics, including sexting, peer exploitation, photo and video sharing, and sexual role-play.

How big is the problem?

One of the most commonly recognized types of grooming is "catfishing." This can happen to anyone on the Internet and is when a person entraps another by pretending to be somebody they're not. We're not taking about people exaggerating their achievements in the way lots of people do when they are dating. This is the creation of an entirely different identity from scratch or stolen from someone else. The motivation can be malicious (as in the case of grooming, or stalking; see p.85) or more innocent (simply an attempt at connection by someone lacking in social and interpersonal skills). It most frequently happens to adults on dating apps or sites, but, when it comes to grooming children, it can occur across many areas of online chatting or social media.

Almost

50%

of children groomed online **WENT ON TO MEET, AND BE EXPLOITED BY,** multiple perpetrators.

WILL'S CASE STUDY

TEENAGE DAUGHTER SUCCESSFULLY GROOMED AND EXPLOITED BY OLDER MAN

One of my clients occasionally confiscates her daughter's phone for bad behavior. However, on one occasion, she became suspicious when her daughter handed it over without the usual fuss. The mother looked in her daughter's schoolbag, where she found a smartphone hidden in a side pocket.

Her daughter had used the same device password as her regular phone, so the mother opened it and found calls from just one number. She also found explicit sext pictures from both her daughter and an adult man.

It is estimated that there are more than 270 million fake accounts on Facebook and 48 million on Twitter. Of these, many are harmless—they might be robots or children under 13 (the age you can legally sign up to Facebook). However, some accounts belong to adults pretending to be children (or even pretending to be teachers or law enforcement) in order to arrange real-life meetups.

How can it affect your family?

It can be devastating because, in many cases, grooming leads to sexual abuse, and it might affect more than one child. While groomers initially set out to create a secret bond between them and one child, and to ensure that the child won't tell their parents, they often try to amass information on other family members, such as siblings, and are likely to share information with other groomers.

Groomers may manipulate children into installing malicious software that enables them to control webcams and other hardware or to give them access to parents' emails. They might persuade the child to enable location tracking that their parents have disabled, to bypass parental controls, or to change passwords to lock their parents out of devices, or to install particular apps or services. Above all, groomers will try to ensure that they have sufficient leverage over the child to prevent them from notifying the police. In some cases, they try to gain leverage over the child's parents, too.

How can you prevent it from happening?

Talk to your child about their friends (real and online). It isn't prying; it's your obligation to keep your child safe. Your child could talk to dozens of people in an hour across various online hangouts. The worry isn't the "five-minute friends" but the people your child talks to most. Ask your child if they have a best online friend. See the box, left, for other suggestions on what to ask your child.

Be wary if specific friends use different apps from everybody else; those people could be trying to stay hidden. Groomers try to separate their target from mainstream chatting platforms into an environment that they control. It's crucial that your child knows not to give out their address or personal information and that they

---

QUESTIONS TO ASK ABOUT YOUR KIDS' ONLINE FRIENDS

Asking your children these questions about their online friends might help you work out whether they are who they say they are:

- Where do they live?
- What do you talk about?
- Where do you talk to them? (i.e., on a site? in a messaging app?)
- Did they approach you, or did you approach them?
- Have they asked to talk on other apps or sites or asked for your phone number or email?
- Have they been talking about real-world meetings?
- Did they ask you a lot of questions about yourself?
- Did they ask anything odd or the kind of thing you'd expect someone much older to ask?
- Did they agree with everything you said?

know they should never agree to meet anybody in secret. If your child wants to meet an online friend in person, they should meet them in public and with you or a trusted adult.

What should you do if it's already happened?

Unfortunately, grooming often isn't discovered until the groomer tries to escalate things into real life. If abuse has already occurred, there might be behavioral changes, from depression or isolation to stealing or self-harming. Or your child may have acquired new clothes, jewelry, or devices. If you notice drastic behavioral changes or unexplained items, check their devices and talk to them.

Avoid judging. Groomers are often very clever and may have been progressively grooming your child over weeks, if not months. If your child has been threatened or abused, they may be in a very dark place, frightened, and worried that there is no way for them to escape their abuser. You need to reassure your child and explain that the more you know, the more you will be able to help.

If you think a groomer has targeted your child, it's crucial to cut off all forms of contact with them and for you to take control, contacting the police if you think it's necessary (see below). It may be appropriate to cancel the account(s) your child has been using and confiscate their devices to ensure there's no further contact.

When should you seek outside help?

If the groomer has talked about sex, has compromising pictures or information, has made threats, or has tried to meet up, contact the police—even if the person has threatened to post compromising material online or threatened to harm a family member. Predators rarely follow through threats. Groomers often target many people at once, and if they fail with one, they'll focus on someone else. Reporting them can stop them from moving on to another child.

Show the relevant device(s) and any other evidence to the police so they can see what's been happening; this can also help them identify the groomer. You can also contact child protection charities. They might be able to provide counseling for your child if required (for resources on who to contact, see p.232).

BEHAVIORAL RED FLAGS

One or more of the following may suggest that your child is being groomed:

- Has an unexplained new device, such as a laptop
- Has expensive new clothing or jewelry
- Undergoes dramatic change in appearance, weight, or behavior
- Is anxious around other grown-ups
- Has become reclusive
- Receives calls and messages from unknown persons and numbers
- Immediately reacts or closes their phone or laptop when you come in the room
- Goes missing from school or home for unexplained periods of time
- Relationships with good friends break down
- Has unexplained physical marks, such as scratches or bruises

PARENTS' QUESTIONS ANSWERED

Will, this is every parent's worst nightmare. How do these people select their targets?

Groomers usually focus on places where they're less likely to get caught: forums, chat rooms, and other more marginal sites that don't check or moderate comments as heavily as the more mainstream, established sites, where they're likely to be detected and reported.

Sometimes they'll think laterally. For example, they might target children in places we don't tend to think of as "the Internet," such as nonconsole-based gaming networks (for example, PC games), especially those with cartoon characters and a chat function. They may hang around forums where people talk about cartoons, again where there's a built-in chat or comments function. They also target people via online shopping sites, especially ones where children can publish "wish lists" that strangers can use to buy them gifts, and even on auction websites.

BUILT-IN CHAT FUNCTIONS on Internet games provide the **PERFECT OPPORTUNITY** for predators to **TARGET** children.

Is there a particular "type" of child they look for?

Predators often target children who appear to be unmonitored —perhaps they're online for long periods of time—or who they believe could be vulnerable. For example, children on the autistic spectrum may be targeted—they can be more trusting because they tend to take things more literally. So if you post articles or links about your child's condition to raise awareness of it, this can have the unintended effect of alerting predators.

What psychological tricks do they use to gain a child's trust?

I mentioned "social engineering" earlier in this chapter—here's an example. Many preteen girls are interested in puppies, kittens, unicorns, pop music, and so on. The groomer might say that they work for a pop band's record company or a toy company or anything else that would have a plausible-sounding reason for wanting to send something to the child. All the child needs to do is give them their address and they'll send them a free gift.

They might offer to share a secret, something like a photo or video that the child has never seen before of their favorite band or a mod for a video game, as long as the child sends them their email address or telephone number.

Or the groomer might share experiences by talking about how uncool or annoying "their" parents are, something that most children can empathize with. They might pretend to be the same age and gender as your child and talk about a boy or girl they supposedly fancy, apparently asking your child for advice but really establishing common ground that the groomer can build on.

This isn't something that just happens overnight. Groomers are very patient, and they tend to plan meticulously. If your child responds to them, they're taking the first step down a very long and very well-planned path prepared for them.

What if my child suspects a person is an imposter, an adult masquerading as someone their age?

Shut down the conversation right away. If they're suspicious or uncomfortable, they need to tell you at once. Check that the site they're on is age appropriate and that your child hasn't pretended to be older. But if the other person knows they're a child, go back online and report the username of the person to the site or service if you can—this could prevent them from contacting any other children in the same way. Under no circumstances should you let your child return to the same site and use it without supervision: first of all, the site clearly

Girls are

9x

more likely than boys to be **TARGETED BY GROOMERS.**

NADIA:
I drum into my girls at every opportunity that. unless they know the person they're talking to online in real life, they can't be sure they are who they say they are.

NADIA:
If my daughter thinks I'm prying, she clams up. So I try to keep conversations general; that way we can talk about difficult topics without her feeling judged.

KAYE:
I've talked about a "friend of a friend" whose child got into trouble online. Then if my daughter gets into hot water, we've started a dialogue, and she might find it easier to confide in me.

doesn't have sufficient protection in place for its users, and second, it's incredibly easy for predators who've been kicked off a site or service to sign up again with a different email address or a completely different identity.

If you're okay with your child continuing to use similar sites or forums after you've reported the offender, make sure your child promises to tell you right away if the person reappears on any other site or with a new account and tries to make contact again. And don't just take your child's word for it: keep an eye on what they're doing and who they're talking to.

Are there specific techniques or certain giveaway phrases they use?

Some techniques are subtly different from how legitimate users chat. For example, unless an online nickname is clearly gender-specific, the first question from a stranger is likely to be "Are you a boy or a girl?" often abbreviated as "M/F?" or "B/G?" Children don't often use the word "sex" to identify someone; someone who does may not be a child.

If the service isn't for a specific age group, the next question may be "How old are you?" and sometimes, "Where are you?" Unless the questioner lives locally, they'll usually be happy with "Miami" or "Columbus"; someone asking for the specific part of town should set red flags flying.

Think about it in terms of the real world: when children meet up in real life, their conversation is full of questions, but these tend to be focused on what they're doing or thinking right now. Children are much more interested in the score another child got in a video game or what a child's favorite Pokémon is than whether Mom and Dad are home.

Another giveaway is persistence. If your child answers questions with short, uninterested answers, most children will give up and move on to someone who's more keen to chat. If the person doesn't, why is this? You wouldn't keep trying to talk to somebody who clearly was not interested; you'd give up. Why aren't they giving up, too?

HOW GROOMERS WORK

Online predators exercise patience and cunningness to draw a victim in. Over time, they'll build trust, developing a relationship in which they may encourage the sharing of secrets that can leave a child vulnerable to manipulation. They will often seek out victims in locations where there are no admins, hosts, or chat monitors (for example, on certain social media sites, comment sections of certain video-sharing sites, or on certain messenger apps). Note that steps 1 and 2 below may not occur in this consequential order.

EXAMPLE GROOMING QUESTIONS

Step 1: Selection
The predator often starts the conversation by trying to determine the age and sex of the child. They may ask directly or steer the conversation to topics relevant to a particular age group and gauge the child's response.

> Hey, what's your name? Where do you go to school? Have you got exams this year?

Step 2: Engagement and alignment
The predator tries to "align" themselves with their potential victim by declaring common or similar likes and interests. They may ask leading questions, using similar language to the child to conceal their true identity, and to encourage the child to reveal their interests with the aim of establishing themselves as a kindred spirit.

> What's your favorite band?
> Me, too, I love them! I saw them last month.

Step 3: Developing friendship
Over time, they try to establish trust. They may compliment the child, offer gifts or rewards, empathize about problems, and share secrets. They may start to suggest that they arrange to meet up in real life.

> My friend knows the band's manager; he can get tickets. We could see them together.

Step 4: Moving to a relationship (the "loving" stage)
By now, the predator has created a "boyfriend/girlfriend" status with their victim. They encourage the child to explore their sexuality, perhaps sharing pornography to desensitize them, and they may try to coerce them into illicit or illegal behaviors, such as keeping secrets from parents, taking drugs, or drinking alcohol, enabling them to have some control over the child.

> I've got a video to show you, but don't let anyone see it. I'd love a picture of you.

Step 5: Manipulation, abuse, and physical contact
Once they have gained the child's trust, or extracted "secrets," they exploit these, using trickery and manipulation if the child doesn't do certain things. They may threaten to disclose secrets, the withdrawal of their friendship or love, or become violent if they have already met up with the child.

> If you don't send me the photo, I'll tell your parents what you've been watching.

How do groomers try to take the "friendship" from online to the real world?

KAYE:
I don't know much about predators, but I know that kids love to be loved! They're so unsure of themselves, always seeking approval, so they're really vulnerable to grooming.

There's often a standard progression. Once the groomer has established common ground, the next step is to create what appears to be a friendship. The groomer then attempts to make that friendship more emotionally intimate, discussing not only topics such as music or games but also feelings and personal experiences. From there, the conversation may be pushed into more sexual territory. All the while, the groomer could be moving toward the goal of a real-life meeting. They might not have moved the conversation into more intimate or sexual areas, but they might feel that they've made enough progress to make a meeting happen.

NADIA:
On a couple of occasions, my children told me about friends making arrangements to meet an online "friend." Both times, I've spoken to the child's parents who convinced them not to go. Phew!

Will they always send a sexually provocative text or selfie first?

It's possible but very rare. Unsolicited, provocative messages are usually from young men or Internet exhibitionists. Groomers tend to be much more subtle—remember, we're talking about very calculating and often very clever people here; they are trying not to scare their potential victims off.

What are the biggest warning signs that I should tell my child to look out for?

Children aren't as tough or as cynical as we are, because usually they haven't needed to be. And, unfortunately, groomers take advantage of that. Behavior that you or I might see as really suspicious might not seem that way to a child. Predators are cunning—they'll constantly change their tactics to avoid being found out.

The key red flags are requests for personal information or suggestions to take the conversation elsewhere—especially somewhere private, such as email or a messaging app.

The question your child should always be asking is "Why?" Why would you want to keep chatting elsewhere when the chat room or site you're on seems fine? Is it to chat privately, to send a video or a game, or to cheat? They need to be suspicious of any suggestions like that.

Your child needs to trust their gut feeling. That feeling that someone or something just isn't right may be the single best ally they have: if your child feels the conversation is getting weird, then it probably is.

If there has already been contact, how do I prevent them from getting access to my child in real life?

Ask your child what they've shared: name, address, pictures, email address, other social media accounts, or telephone number. You need to know what avenues the predator might have to contact your child and close these off. You also need to contact the police—to protect not only your child but also other children who they and their accomplices may target.

If the contact has been in a chat room, contact the administrators (if there are any), and report the behavior. If there aren't administrators, delete the account (screenshot conversations first for evidence; see p.227). Your child must understand that they can't use that site or service again.

If you think the groomer is aware of your child's other social media accounts and you know the identity the groomer uses on those services, block and report them. If you can't, delete your child's vulnerable accounts and recreate them with good usernames (see p.36) and privacy settings (pp.200–217).

If the contact has been via email, set up a new account for your child (without an easily guessable address that's similar to the existing one) and take over the old account yourself. Any future emails will then come to you, and you can forward them to the relevant authorities.

If the contact has been via phone, don't just rely on its Block Contact feature. The groomer can have a new pay-as-you-go phone with a different number in seconds. Get a new

It can take
LESS THAN

30

MINUTES
for an online
groomer to
PERSUADE
a child to
meet them.

SIM card with a new phone number, and make sure your child shares the new number with only people you both know you can trust. If your child's phone, laptop, or the family desktop has records of contacts—received messages or emails or chat logs—keep them.

Will the police investigate, and what else can we do to help them find the groomer?

The police take reports of grooming seriously. Grooming is a major offense, and the people who do it have a great deal to lose if they're caught. Many groomers are part of wider networks that the police may already be working on bringing to justice.

First, screenshot any evidence (see p.227). If the person has reason to believe they've been found out, they'll try to cover their tracks. Don't assume that the site keeps copies of messages or images that have been deleted by the groomer. Keep any emails and images or videos (as long as they don't contain pornographic images of minors—having such images on a device is illegal and can result in criminal prosecution).

In most cases, the groomer will have one or more usernames (expect "Videogamedude1337" rather than "Dave Johnson from 134 Green Street"). Most services enable you to report bad or worrying behavior with nothing more than the username, but if you're going to the police, it's worth checking the person's profile page to see whether they've given extra information, such as a link to another social media account.

It's really important that you follow the steps I've outlined in "It's All Gone Wrong" (pp.218–227), which explains how to find out and store essential information, such as where the emails have really been sent from. And make sure you record not only what happened but also when it happened. Most electronic communications, from text messages to forum posts, are stamped with the date they were sent or posted. This is all useful information for the police.

TAKEAWAYS

1 DENY A GROOMER CONTACT Talk to your child about how groomers operate and that they may try to arrange a real-life meet.

2 BE SUSPICIOUS OF PERSONAL QUESTIONS AND GIFTS Explain to your child how a groomer may try to gain trust and information (see social engineering, p.103).

3 TALK TO YOUR CHILD Know who your child is communicating with regularly online.

4 TELL YOUR CHILD TO TRUST THEIR INSTINCTS Talk to your child about trusting their gut—if they feel questions are odd/too probing, sign off.

5 DON'T SHARE PERSONAL DETAILS Tell your child to never reveal their full name, phone number, address, or other usernames or social media accounts to online strangers.

6 TELL YOUR CHILD TO BE HONEST ABOUT THEIR AGE Lying about their age online could dupe an innocent person and cause complications.

7 WATCH OUT FOR GROOMERS EVERYWHERE Not just in chat rooms—they can be friends of friends, on online gaming, or anywhere else online.

8 DON'T HESITATE TO REPORT A GROOMER If there's been contact, a groomer may have gained information on siblings, parents, friends, and extended family and shared that information with other groomers.

9 CLOSE DOWN AVENUES OF CONTACT If you suspect grooming, block and/or delete your child's account, and report what has happened to the police.

WANT MORE INFO? If this chapter hasn't answered all your questions, try:

- Top Things Not to Share Online, p.36
- Chatting Online, pp.36–45
- Cyberstalking, pp.85–87

SEXTING

THE DANGERS OF INTIMATE TEXTS AND NUDE PHOTOS

WHAT YOU NEED TO KNOW

NADIA'S EXPERIENCE

Even though it turns me gray every time I do it, sexting is something my daughter Maddie and I often talk—ugh—frankly about. It seems one of the most common experiences of sexting for her girlfriends is to receive anonymous "dick pics" (yes, I had the same shudder when I heard those words) in the form of direct messages.

When I plead with Maddie to help me understand why her friends don't just have private accounts in order to avoid this modern-day form of flashing, she says that many of her friends feel a sense of empowerment in being able to look and laugh. In fact, some girls see those visual "assaults" (as I call them) as opportunities to turn the tables on those who send them.

Maddie tells me that she knows lots of girls who have sent nude images of themselves only to make the horrifying discovery that the boy they sent them to then passed them around his entire friendship group. One can only imagine the mortification this must cause these poor girls.

So, in a strange form of feminist revenge, some girls have taken to screenshotting these dick pics (which, on some platforms, informs the sender that a screenshot has been taken) and using them as leverage against the sender.

Of course, my husband and I would much rather friends of Maddie weren't seeing these images at all, and, I have to confess, I never cease to be amazed at how receiving a dick pic is often accompanied by laughter. It seems that a desensitization of what is right or wrong to see on your mobile device has already occurred, so there is virtually no shock attached to seeing such abusive images.

In fact, the idea of female empowerment appears to be a huge part of sexting. The argument seems to be that the sender of nude photos, by "being in demand" or "being in control" of how they

Up to
20%
of teens have sent or posted a **SEMINUDE OR FULL-NUDE** image online.

are seen on-screen, is somehow in control of how they're seen by their social group. These justifications of sexting or sending sexualized images are a grave cause for concern for any parent.

WILL'S EXPERT ANALYSIS

Sexually provocative messages ("sexts") and images are now part of flirtation and conversation in romantic relationships, or prospective ones, but messages and images can be used maliciously for coercion, bullying, or even, if a relationship turns sour, revenge (see box, below). Over the last 10 years, I have heard an increasing number of stories about sexting from distraught parents and, on occasion, from children themselves.

Sometimes, however, a sext is sent simply as a bit of fun, to get attention from peers or a specific individual, or for pure shock value. As adults, we need to remember that teenagers see a lot more sexual and sexualized content than many of us do. To them, it's just what everybody does. Although we can't change this new "normal," we can guide our kids through it.

How big is the problem?

Across the world, the statistics are pretty uniform, with boys and girls almost equal in sending sexually explicit messages, but boys send more photographs of themselves. What's really frightening is how young the children are. Many are 13 or 14, and

40% of teens will send a sext message **AS A JOKE.**

WILL'S CASE STUDY

TEENAGE GIRL IS SUBJECTED TO DOZENS OF UNWELCOME SEXUALLY EXPLICIT IMAGES

I advised a father who was contacted by another extremely irate parent. Apparently, his son had sent loads of pornographic pictures and sexually abusive messages to the parent's daughter after she had rejected the son's requests to go on a date. The father had been completely unaware of what his son had been doing. He had the unenviable task of confronting him and explaining the potentially serious repercussions.

some are much younger. Nearly half of older kids say that they expect other people to see privately shared photos.

We all tend to think, "There's no way my child would do something like that," but 6 out of 10 older children have sent a sext, and 2 out of 10 have sent nude images. And those numbers are increasing every year.

How could it affect your family?

It is all too easy for a sext or image to be shared far beyond the intended recipient. At best, there's the embarrassment of your child's messages being circulated among their friends, but that can easily escalate to their friends' brothers and sisters, teachers, parents, or, even worse, total strangers. In some circumstances, sending explicit messages or images can be viewed as sexual harassment if a person isn't receptive to receiving it or finds it offensive. And an image that was sent during a relationship may be used as "revenge porn" if the relationship ends badly, which in many countries is now a criminal offense. Most seriously, images could land you or your child in deep trouble: making, possessing, or circulating sexual images of anybody under the age of consent is a serious criminal offense.

How do you prevent it from happening?

You can randomly check your child's phone (I'd recommend following the steps we've described in the "Device Safety and Security" chapter; see pp.200–217), but most importantly you need to help them understand the risks and consequences.

Ask them to consider who the end viewer (or viewers) could be and how much they trust the person they are sending it to. Would they send the text message or nude selfie if they knew it would be seen by a family member, posted on social media, or sent around their school?

What should you do if it's already happened?

With something like this, unfortunately coming to you is probably your child's very last resort. When they do, offer reassurance and support, not recriminations; tell them you're a team. First, try to

---

KAYE:
I can go quite Victorian at the thought of my girls sending or receiving a sext, but let's take a deep breath—whether we like it or not, the teenage years are when they develop as sexual beings.

WHERE DID YOUR SEXT GO?

There are many ways that a sext or image can travel without your child's permission. These include:

- Using an incorrect email address or phone number

- The recipient taking a screenshot of the image

- Someone seeing the image on the recipient's device over their shoulder

- A device containing the image being left unlocked

- A device containing the image backing up to another connected device, shared network, cloud, or server (at home, school, or work)

- The recipient sharing the image on social media or phone to phone to bully or embarrass the sender, or as an act of "revenge porn."

find out who has a copy of the sext or image and, if it's an image, whether it has been put on social media. If it's the latter, the big social media services have tools for reporting unauthorized images in their "Help" sections. If your child has been tagged, they may even be able to delete the image themselves. Otherwise, notify anyone who has the image that they need to delete it and take down any posts containing it at once. Take a screenshot of all your requests for removal—you may need them later. If your child is under 18, make it clear to others that possessing or sharing the image is a criminal offense and that you will go to the police if the image isn't removed.

When should you seek outside help?

If there are adults involved, if you think the image has spread widely, or if your requests for removal have been ignored, then it's time to get serious.

To do that, first, you need to know all the details—a description of the image or text, the time it was sent, and to whom (or where it was posted)—so you can decide how serious the situation is and whether you need to get other parents, the school, or the police involved. Don't be scared to report this to the police; you could be protecting not only your own child but also other children.

DECIPHERING SEXTING

These key acronyms will help you to understand what your children's messages mean.

143 I love you

182 I hate you

53X Sex

8 Oral sex

CU46 See you for sex

GNOC Get naked on camera

GYPO Get your pants off

HAK Hugs and kisses

IPN I'm posting naked

IWSN I want sex now

JO Jerking off

KOTL Kiss on the lips

LMIRL Let's meet in real life

NIFOC Naked in front of computer

PAL Parents are listening

PIR Parent in room

POS Parent over shoulder

PRON Porn

SUGARPIC Suggestive or erotic pic

TDTM Talk dirty to me

WTTP Want to trade pictures?

PARENTS' QUESTIONS ANSWERED

> **My daughter has been receiving some pretty risqué text messages from a boy at school, but what started as a bit of banter has become much more persistent. It feels like sexual harassment—is it?**

Sexual harassment is any unwelcome written, verbal, or physical comments, attention, or contact. While laws vary in different countries, if your daughter is receiving text messages she finds objectionable and which are persistent, and he doesn't de-escalate his language or stop completely after she tells him to stop, he is harassing her.

But she did engage with him at the start; is this a problem for her?

It's important for any victim to know that it is not their fault and that they don't in some way "deserve" it. If your daughter was making her first tentative steps at flirting, for example, and it then went awry, it doesn't negate the fact that what is happening now is harassment. People can sometimes be bolder or have looser boundaries on the Internet, so it's worth talking to her about setting her own boundaries of what she finds acceptable and making these clear to everyone she engages with. If something doesn't feel right to her, she must follow her gut feeling.

What can she do to stop it?

As soon as the text messaging has breached her comfort level, she should immediately tell him to stop. It could be that he's quite innocently made an error of judgment, and this should

Just under

50%

of teens say they have received **SEXUALLY SUGGESTIVE**— sometimes **UNWELCOME**— messages.

then result in an apology from him and no further offense caused. He may still be new to flirting himself, or he may have genuinely misread her signals.

What if he won't stop?

Some individuals are more manipulative and may be doing it as a means of intimidation, bullying, or aggression. If this type of serious harassment persists and/or escalates, report it to the police. Even if the police don't have grounds to prosecute, try to insist that they contact the perpetrator and issue a "harassment" warning, which is a precursor to more formal charges. This might be enough to make the boy stop.

NADIA:
I'm sure this is terribly un-PC, but when my daughter was being hassled online by a rather unsavory fellow, my husband intervened by messaging him, warning him off. It worked a treat!

When checking my son's laptop, I found photos that I think are of a girl from his school. Should I confront him about this?

If your son knows that you check his laptop, he will be aware that you can find things, so do confront him. Talk to him rationally and without accusation at first. Ask him who she is. Does he know her? Did she send them to him? Then explain to him the embarrassment and legal risks (see p.104), not only for her but also for him for possessing them, and that, for both their sakes, it is best he deletes the images.

KAYE:
Of course, teenagers have a right to a private life, but they need to be aware in no uncertain terms of the potential dangers and repercussions.

If the pictures are of someone who is underage, he must delete them immediately or he could get into trouble with the police—even if she sent them to him. In fact, she could get in as much trouble for distributing them as he could for having them on his device. This is because the authorities treat any nude photos of someone underage as "child pornography."

THE YOUNGEST RECORDED INCIDENT
of sexting involved a 5-YEAR-OLD child

What are the potential repercussions?

This is very serious. In most parts of the world, it's a criminal offense to possess indecent images of anybody under 18 or to incite them to engage in sexual activity (soliciting an explicit photo falls under the latter).

A child taking a nude selfie is unlikely to be charged, but receiving and keeping a nude selfie of a friend could lead to prosecution. It doesn't even matter if your son is also underage; what matters when it comes to prosecution is the age of criminal responsibility where you live. This varies from country to country; for example, in the US, this could be as low as age 11, depending on which state you live in. The age is 10 in England and Australia and 12 in Scotland and Canada.

What if my son is 18 or older and shares images with a younger girl?

If your son is 18 or older, the issue becomes even more serious since, if the police get involved, he will be prosecuted as an adult possessing indecent images of a child. This is still the case even if the images were received before he turned 18.

This means the police turning up at your house with warrants to seize and search his devices for any other illegal material. If they prosecute and they're successful, he could be given up to 10 years in prison and a lifetime on the Sex Offenders' registry, meaning he may struggle to get a job and face restrictions on where he can live for the rest of his life. If there's media coverage, the online record could ruin his future employment and relationship prospects.

Even if the case doesn't go to court, his arrest for a child sex offense will permanently stay on his record. If he wants to visit certain countries, go to college, or do anything that requires declaring any police record, he'll need to explain it. People often jump to conclusions when they hear "child sex offense"—they don't tend to think of teenagers sharing risqué photos.

Sometimes teenagers just don't listen when they hear "no." Some kids are clearly going to send risqué selfies anyway. Is there any advice you think they'd actually listen to?

You're right: you can tell children not to do it, but you can't really stop them. However, you can talk to your child about the dangers of sexting and make sure you have this conversation whenever you give them any device that is capable of taking and sending photographs. When doing this, bear in mind the earlier section on how to talk to your child about technology (see pp.12–21).

For older children, I think it's important to use "harm reduction" tactics, as outlined on p.120. Think of it like alcohol—they'll probably be tempted or pressured by their peers, and warning them about the risks isn't necessarily going to stop them from trying something, but providing these tactics will reduce the chance of things going horribly wrong if they succumb to that peer pressure.

NADIA:
I'm hoping that I have terrified my girls enough with the shock-horror stories I've found in newspapers of when sexting has gone wrong that they're never tempted themselves. Fingers crossed!

If my child's image is shared without his permission, is there any way to tell who has leaked it?

Actually, yes, there is. Your child can add a watermark to the image that has the recipient's name. This will mean that the image can't be copied, shared, duplicated, or altered without showing the recipient's name marked across it, so it offers a form of protection for the sender. It is illegal to distribute private and personal images without the owner's consent, so if this happens, the watermark can be used by the police for criminal prosecution.

It's easy to add a watermark. You can use the Preview program on Apple or the Paint option on Windows to add an identifying mark; there are also plenty of sources on the Internet that will show how to do this.

HARM REDUCTION

Simple tricks will help keep a selfie incognito and limit the ability of others to identify or trace it. These are examples of selfies with and without harm reduction.

1 Full face is visible but could be cropped out or in shadow.

2 Identifying marks such as birthmarks could be covered up.

3 Hands could be hidden.

4 Distinctive clothing and accessories could be removed.

5 Background could be kept neutral and free of clues.

40% of teenage girls admit to **PARTICIPATING IN SEXTING AS A JOKE**, 34% did it to feel sexy, and 12% felt **PRESSURED** to do it.

What does harm reduction involve?

It means concealing your child's identity in photos (see box, above). Ideally, though, I wouldn't usually endorse searching for this online; they should use an image of a stranger. They can find one with a similar body shape and with no identifying features. Otherwise, they should hide their face, angle the camera below their neck, avoid showing their hands, hide body markings (moles or birthmarks as well as tattoos), and remove anything indentifying in the background.

If the image is shared, they can't be embarrassed, blackmailed, or bullied about it.

Isn't harm reduction saying, "Do it; I don't care"?

Not at all. It's saying you don't want your child to get hurt. Harm reduction is important, but I'd also tell your child to consider where their photo could end up. If parents, siblings, friends, future lovers, and potential employers can find it on the Internet, it could embarrass them for the rest of their life. Seriously, is it really worth it?

TAKEAWAYS

1 THINK ABOUT THE MOTIVATION BEHIND A SEXT Identifying why a sext was sent—as a "test" to prove trust, to seek validation or approval, or for pure shock value—can help to deal with it.

2 KNOW ABOUT THE CRIMINAL REPERCUSSIONS Sexting is illegal under the age of consent. Tell recipients of a nude image of your child to delete it and ask any website to take it down.

3 SPELL OUT THE DANGERS OF IMAGE SHARING TO YOUR CHILD Make sure your child knows that being in possession of or sharing, explicit images of anyone underage is a crime in most countries.

4 OFFER SUPPORT, NOT PUNISHMENT Make sure your child knows that they can come to you for help—they don't have to deal with a bad situation alone. There may be many reasons why they sent it.

5 CONSIDER HARM REDUCTION If a child ignores advice not to send a compromising image, talk to them about concealing their identity or sending a fake picture to avoid future embarrassment.

6 SEEK SUPPORT FOR HARASSMENT Contact the organizations and charities listed on p.232 for support if your child is being harassed or is receiving unwanted sexts or nude images.

WANT MORE INFO? If this chapter hasn't answered all your questions, try:

- Pornography and Violent Content, pp.124–127
- Behavioral Warning Signs, p.17, p.126
- Self-esteem, p.52
- Selfies, pp.54–55
- Top Things Not to Share Online, p.36

PORNOGRAPHY AND VIOLENT CONTENT

GUIDING KIDS AWAY FROM EXTREME MATERIAL ONLINE

WHAT YOU NEED TO KNOW

NADIA'S EXPERIENCE

One of the things that has most distressed me over the years involved my daughter Maddie seeing something that was entirely beyond our, or her, control. In fact, she wasn't even using a computer or a smartphone herself!

When she was at school and about 11 years old, during lunch break, one of her friends thought it would be funny to shock everyone by clicking on a clip of someone being beheaded by a terrorist and thrusting it into everyone's faces. The horror of seeing such a thing couldn't be avoided as Maddie was given no choice as to whether or not to watch it. Soldiers who return from wars can sometimes require long-term counseling due to scenes of horror like this—how have we gotten to a point where seeing such graphic and disturbing images is something that just "can happen" and that your kid can come home from school and say, "I saw someone being beheaded"? The availability of these clips is desensitizing our youngsters to the horrific violence they show.

This effect of adult content on youngsters was really brought home to me, and especially my husband, Mark, when we spoke to his eldest daughter's boyfriend, who described the ways in which hard-core porn and its availability online was creating huge pressures and confusion in young men. He would describe the ways in which boys he knew would find ever more explicit and extreme content in an attempt to outdo each other and would then share it to shock each other. They would then challenge each other to try the stuff they'd seen people doing online. He said that many of his friends just didn't know about boundaries when it came to flirting or sex and that most boys were in a fog of intimidation (caused by the footage). They also had a deep misunderstanding of what was "normal" in a sexual relationship, because ideas of what might be acceptable had been so monumentally blurred by porn.

90%

of kids from as young as 8 to 16 years old have WATCHED PORNOGRAPHY ONLINE AT LEAST ONCE.

WILL'S EXPERT ANALYSIS

We're all aware of how accessible porn is, but it's not the only inappropriate stuff being shared online, sometimes even in apps designed for children. YouTube has had problems with clips being added to its kids channels showing popular children's cartoon characters being attacked, stabbed, or even buried alive—and that's in what is supposedly the "safe" part of the Internet, specifically geared to children. There are entire websites showcasing stomach-churning videos of real-life violence and gore. Extreme adult material on the Internet is never more than a search away, and, even with parental controls switched on, it's easy to encounter explicit content without intending to. I think we're resigned to the fact that if a child wants to find extreme content online, they'll find it (or somebody will find it for them).

There's a dictum in my business, "What is seen can never be unseen." We need to prepare children for the possibility of finding this horrific content and the impact it could have on them and teach them how to reduce the chances of it happening.

How big is the problem?

The majority of teenagers are thought to have watched online pornography, and more than a quarter of young people have had it sent to them by other people—usually by other children. You may be able to put parental controls on the devices in your family, but

FATHER DISCOVERS EXTREME PORN CONTENT HIDDEN IN SON'S BOGUS CALCULATOR APP

A father called me for advice about multiple "CryptLocker" accounts he had found on his son's device. He had no idea what they were. I explained that these were file-sharing websites that often contain illegal downloads of music, movies, software, and other, usually illegal, material. The father called back to say he had accessed the sites via his son's device and found huge quantities of extreme porn that his son had been downloading and sharing daily for months then storing in an app masquerading as a calculator.

KAYE:
Here's how easy it is to access online porn. I googled "Victorian maids" to help my youngest with a school project. The stuff that came up would make you blanch—time to upgrade those parental controls!

you can't do this for laptops and smartphones belonging to friends. Your child can encounter explicit or extreme material when they're searching for something else, on online forums, on messaging apps, on music download sites, by being sent or shown it by friends, or by receiving it from complete strangers on social networks.

How could it affect your family?

The biggest risk to your family is likely to be how it could affect your child's behavior. Your child might start using words they know they shouldn't or start asking about adult-related subjects they haven't previously spoken about. You might hear them using offensive language with other children, asking inappropriate questions, or "acting out" by behaving in attention-seeking ways. Even if this behavior doesn't cause them trouble at school, it can affect your child's social relationships and view of the opposite sex.

And that brings us to another concern, which is that, for some children, pornography becomes their primary form of sexual education. Nearly half of 12- to 16-year-olds say they want to try out things they've seen people do in online porn.

How do you prevent it from happening?

The problem with explicit and extreme content is that taking it off the Internet or preventing children from seeing it is like playing Whac-A-Mole—close down one site, and another one appears in its place. Parental controls can help, but children, especially older ones, can often find ways to get around controls and then hide the material that they've downloaded, sometimes on a friend's device.

You should periodically check your child's browsing history and watch for signs that they are trying to hide what they've been looking at (see right). Think of the Internet like the real world: often the best thing you can do is just talk to your kids and encourage them to share anything they've seen that has confused or upset them.

What should you do if it's already happened?

You need to find out why your child was viewing that material. Did they find it on their own, or did someone share it? Tell your child

BEHAVIORAL RED FLAGS

Boys and girls may exhibit some of the following behaviors if they've viewed extreme material:

• Suddenly becoming disrespectful and dismissive

• Starting to act in an aggressive or agitated way

• Making flippant or callous remarks about human or animal suffering

• Dressing out of character, for example, by dressing much more provocatively

• Suddenly trying to appear more grown-up, for example, by using makeup

• New or increased narcissistic or attention-seeking behavior

• Talking disrespectfully and sexually about girls and women

it's normal to be curious but that there are dangers to viewing some of the material they might find—not just the legal risks, but the risk of seeing things they can't unsee. And, of course, in the case of pornography, you need to explain to your child the huge difference between real sex and pornographic sex. You might want to approach this conversation using the advice given on p.16.

The next step really depends on their reaction. If your child is flippant or disregards what you're saying, I'd digitally ground them (that means no phone, computer, or tablet) and set conditions for the grounding to be lifted. Stress that it's about protecting them, not punishing them—if they can prove to you that they can be trusted, they'll get their gadgets back. While you can't stop them from getting online elsewhere, this will stop them from viewing material at home and perhaps convey the severity of the situation.

When should you seek outside help?

The biggest danger here is illegal content. The definition of that varies from country to country, but as a rule of thumb, pornography involving anybody under 18, or that contains violence or any sort of nonconsensual sexual activity, is illegal to possess or distribute. If you find content of this nature on their device, it needs to be deleted immediately (remember to empty your Trash folder, too).

If your child is repeatedly visiting websites containing extreme or illegal material and they're ignoring your advice or instructions, then you'll need to consider more drastic action. There are third parties that can help: child charity helplines can be really useful, and you might be able to get support from a child counselor. If your child is showing signs of addictive behavior, it may be appropriate to get them referred for counseling and support.

Entering "SEX" into the Google search bar produces more than **817 MILLION** results.

TELLTALE SIGNS

Any of the following signs could mean that your child is trying to hide something they've been looking at:

● They constantly clear their browsing history, or their search history appears suspiciously empty (they could be using "private browsing" to access material without leaving any browsing history)

● They've installed a new app that appears to be something else, such as a calculator (this can be a good hiding place)

● They have photo galleries, files, or apps on their device that are password protected

PARENTS' QUESTIONS ANSWERED

My son has downloaded a lot of porn—and I mean a lot. I don't know what to do.

> **KAYE:**
> I might have a level of control over pornographic content in my own home, but I don't kid myself that my daughters won't be exposed to it elsewhere.

It's hard to strike the balance here. We know that children become curious about sex and that many—maybe most—will see pornography either by accident or on purpose. The point to worry is when the pornography your son is viewing includes illegal or extreme content, or if it's leading to worrying behavior (e.g., hoarding large numbers of images.)

How do I approach him?

Talk to him, but don't be angry. Say you want to understand why he downloaded so much pornography. He'll most likely be mortified. The second thing is to explain that porn is like action movies or video games—just because it's on screen doesn't mean it's realistic. It's fantasy for adults, not an instruction manual for children. If he does what people do in pornography, he may upset others and drive them away.

What should we do with all this content? Can it still exist on his hard drive even if we delete it?

Delete the porn (making sure to delete it from the Trash folder, too) and issue a warning that you will cut off his Internet access if he downloads it again. The material may still exist on his hard drive even if you delete, it, but he won't be able to access it unless he has certain recovery software. It's more likely that he will simply download the same material again if he wants to rebuild the collection of files that has been deleted. If he continues to download large amounts of extreme or illegal material, you could confiscate his device and perhaps call in a counselor to talk to him.

How can I monitor his viewing?

One compromise could be to not use Internet filters but to say that he isn't allowed to clear his browsing history daily or empty his trash/recycling bin (or that only you can), and let him know you might have a look at any time. There are tips online on how to check the time and date of when a bin has been emptied. The message is clear: you're trusting him to be sensible about what he views, but if that trust is broken, you'll lock down his Internet access so it's suitable only for toddlers.

> **I'm not worried about my daughter watching porn. I'm worried about the kids watching porn who want to date my daughter. What weird ideas are they getting?**

I think we have to give our kids the benefit of the doubt here. Just because there's really offensive and often degrading pornography out there doesn't mean that everybody's viewing that stuff, let alone trying to reenact it. But, that said, you should prepare your daughter for the worst-case scenario.

How do I prepare her?

Talk frankly and openly to your daughter about what's normal, what isn't, and what's completely unacceptable. Most importantly, let her know that when it comes to sexual matters, "no" means "no" and that she should never feel pressured into doing anything she isn't comfortable with.

NADIA:
I regularly talk to my daughters about how to evaluate material they might be exposed to online. It's important for parents of sons to have similar chats.

KAYE:
I agree. We need to have conversations about the differences between pornography and healthy sex.

Regardless of what her friends say, she should always take things at her own pace and set her own thresholds of what she finds acceptable. If she is unsure about anything, she should talk to you or another trusted adult.

> **My son and his friends share really horrific, gory stuff. Should I be worried that this will make them more violent or aggressive?**

This isn't a new concern; people have been worrying about violent content in films and video games since the 1980s. Nobody has come up with a definitive answer, so let's opt for a common-sense approach.

There's such a thing as "desensitization," which is where what used to shock someone doesn't shock them anymore. For example, a child might share a graphic video from the Internet, and then, when that's no longer shocking, they might find a clip that's a bit worse and then another that's worse again. This escalation can result in children seeing some pretty diabolical things.

So what can I do to stop him from looking at this stuff?
The best thing you can do is to convince him that this isn't stuff he wants to see and that he won't be able to unsee what he's seen. Looking at this material is potentially damaging to him. He could be scared or have nightmares, and, if the material is illegal, he could get in trouble with the authorities.

It's also worth impressing upon him that it's not just about him; he could be inflicting trauma on his friends. Just because he is not scared of something doesn't mean that someone else won't be. It's almost impossible to know when you might be

Almost
30%
of children aged 11–16 have SEEN ADULT CONTENT BY ACCIDENT in a pop-up window.

crossing that line for someone else. Stress to him that for this reason, it's not appropriate to show other kids these sorts of graphic videos.

I've noticed he's become a bit more confrontational. Is this a sign of what he's viewing or just because I'm asking about it?

If your son is acting at all aggressively, you need to find the cause (which could be online or offline). Check his search history to see if he's consuming a lot of violent or aggressive content. One worry is trauma. The worst content online can give you nightmares for a long time. If you have concerns about his mental health, seek help from the professionals.

Is it illegal to view as well as to own?

There are a lot of similarities between extreme content and pornography, not least that some of it is illegal. If there's awful stuff on his devices, it must be deleted (unless you need to use it as evidence; see pp.222–225). If he has been actively seeking out content that contains the mistreatment of animals or people, have a serious conversation emphasizing the illegality of the content and perhaps suggest counseling.

There are lots of pop-ups with explicit images appearing on my child's computer. Should I be concerned? How can I stop them from appearing?

Explicit pop-ups tend to appear in the "bad" parts of the Internet, such as file-sharing or illegal streaming websites or when visiting horrible websites. You can install ad blockers, but some sites demand you turn this software off before any material is viewed, and many pop-ups can bypass ad blockers.

So should I tell my kids to stay off these sites?

Yes. Impress upon them the danger that they might see something they can't unsee in pop-ups or by downloading a file labeled as something innocent. They also risk accidentally downloading malware or a virus, which would prevent them from watching anything at all. Since explicit pop-ups don't appear on sites that require paid subscriptions, such as Netflix or Amazon Prime, you might want to pay for an online streaming subscription. You can then offer your child a safe alternative to the illegal sites.

Good Internet security software from a trusted developer will warn you before you enter a site that it is a security risk or may contain malicious pop-ups.

APPS THAT HIDE

Some apps can be a cover for accessing and hiding material, such as pornography. Monitor your child's app purchases regularly and ask them about new apps and what they do. Here, a seemingly innocent calculator app is actually a folder containing hidden photos and videos.

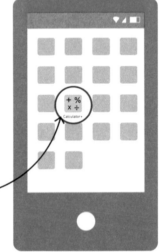

From the outside, the app appears to be something innocent, such as a calculator or utilities folder.

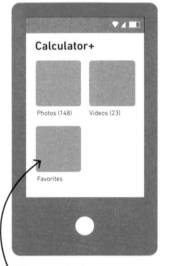

When you enter the app, you find it is actually a hiding place for images and videos.

TAKEAWAYS

1 BUILD TRUST Keep communication open, and let your child know they can discuss anything upsetting or disturbing they see.

2 CHECK THEIR BROWSING HISTORY AND APPS Look for suspicious downloads, empty browsing history, or suspicious new apps that suggest your child is hiding their online viewing.

3 TALK ABOUT REAL-LIFE RELATIONSHIPS Explain how porn isn't a realistic presentation of sex or relationships.

4 STRESS THAT WHAT IS SEEN CAN'T BE UNSEEN Nasty content can stay with you, causing distress, nightmares, and even depression.

5 BE AWARE OF WHAT'S ILLEGAL Extreme material can be illegal; make sure your child is aware that possession can land them a criminal conviction.

6 LOOK FOR BEHAVIORAL INDICATORS Are they using explicit language, initiating conversations on adult themes, or acting out in order to shock others?

7 REMIND YOUR CHILD THAT EVERYTHING LEAVES A TRACE Make them aware that there are ways to recover their viewing history (such as checking the cookies listed in the web browser privacy settings).

8 ACCEPT YOUR CHILD WILL VIEW UNSUITABLE MATERIAL Children are curious and may actively search for this kind of content. Understanding this can help you deal with it calmly.

9 CONSIDER COUNSELING If your child refuses to stop viewing extreme or illegal material, or shows addictive behavior, remove devices and contact a counselor.

WANT MORE INFO? If this chapter hasn't answered all your questions, try:

COERCION, EXTORTION, AND BLACKMAIL

HOW TO DEAL WITH THREATS AND DEMANDS

WHAT YOU NEED TO KNOW

KAYE'S EXPERIENCE

When you've worked as a journalist for as long as I have (more than 25 years), it takes a lot to shock you. But, once in a while, a story comes along that cracks your shell, invariably because it makes you think: "I could find myself and my family in a similar situation."

It was a few years back, when the online world was even more uncharted territory than it is now. A 17-year-old boy who lived not far from my home took his own life, apparently out of the blue.

It wasn't until the police got hold of his computer that it was discovered that he had fallen victim to a gang of blackmailers, most likely based thousands of miles away in the Philippines. He didn't know that; he thought he had struck up a romance with a girl his own age. They chatted online fairly innocently for weeks before she asked him to send her intimate pictures of himself. That was the moment he got caught in a web from which he just couldn't untangle himself.

Demands for money followed, along with threats to expose him to his family and coworkers. They kept coming and coming. He couldn't pay, and he couldn't face the humiliation, and, ultimately, he took the only way out he could think of.

His family were torn apart.

I couldn't help but think of my own girls and of my teenage self. It's a time of life when everything matters, emotions are heightened, and embarrassment causes actual physical pain. The alleged gang was tracked down but never brought to justice. They were not much older than their victim. Destitute and desperate, they had no care for the consequences of their actions. They just wanted money and had tried the same tactics on countless numbers of random teenagers.

According to an FBI report,

71%

of **SEXTORTION VICTIMS** in the US are **UNDER 18**.

WILL'S EXPERT ANALYSIS

Online extortion has become much more common over the last couple of decades. It ranges from the sophisticated—hackers holding companies to ransom for tens of millions—to ransomware that locks up laptops until you pay up; so-called ethical hacking, where a system is hacked without the owner's consent to expose vulnerabilities and then offer to fix them for a fee; and "sextortion," where a hacker steals intimate photos or tricks the victim into sending them. The motivation isn't always financial; it can be to damage someone's character, gain revenge because of a personal grudge, sexually abuse them, or even force them to commit a crime.

A lot of this crime goes unreported because victims are ashamed, feel stupid, or feel it's their fault. That's a false belief. Somebody has abused the victim's trust. And sometimes they don't report it because they've been told that if they do, the blackmailer will share their photos or data and destroy their reputation. That's a horrible threat for anybody but particularly for children, who may feel more distressed at the prospect of being shamed in front of their peers.

Anybody can be targeted: rich, poor, young, old, male, or female. But don't despair. There are lots of things you can do to protect yourself and your family and lots that victims can do to fight back.

WILL'S CASE STUDY

GIRL BLACKMAILED WITH FAKE PORN PICS OF HER BY AN ONLINE STRANGER

Some clients of mine discovered that their daughter had been quietly selling all her possessions without them realizing. They were concerned it might have been to obtain cash for a drug habit. However, when she eventually disclosed the real reason she needed the cash, they were even more shocked. She had been approached online by a stranger who had accessed her social media account and created fake pornographic images of her. The photos looked very convincing, and she was terrified. Unless she sent money, the stranger threatened that they would send the images to her friends, teachers, and even family.

KAYE:
I'll be honest: I zone out at the mention of security software and settings. I bought a Mac because someone told me you didn't need antivirus software for them. Will, I now assume that's wrong?

WILL:
Yes, every device is vulnerable these days. Always install antivirus and antimalware software and download all the updates for it.

TECH SECURITY DO'S AND DON'TS

Protect your devices with these safety practices:

● **Do** regularly update all software and security settings.

● **Don't** use easy-to-guess passwords and use different ones for different accounts.

● **Do** have up-to-date antivirus software on all your computers.

● **Do** run antivirus checks on downloads before you open them, even from sites you trust.

● **Don't** automatically trust official-looking emails from banks, software providers, and other firms. These could be phishing attacks (see p.162).

How big is the problem?

It's global. Someone on the other side of the world could try to coerce your child into revealing information that could be used to blackmail them. Sextortion is on the rise in Europe and forms part of a wider trend of global cybercrime and organized crime involving ransoms that law enforcement agencies (such as the FBI and Europol) are concerned about.

How could it affect your family?

In all the cases I've been involved with, the impact has been severe: embarrassment, financial problems, psychological damage, and even self-harm. It can lead to other family members being targeted, the family computer frozen or corrupted, loss of possessions, and bank accounts being emptied. If your child has been targeted, alert other family members to avoid them being caught up in the scam.

How do you prevent it from happening?

Without up-to-date security software and robust security settings, ransomware and other malicious software can easily get into a computer (see also pp.206–209). Educate your child about the dangers of visiting file-sharing sites for music, movies, or games: many of those downloads can be packed with hidden viruses.

What's on the computer your child uses? If it got infected or was hacked, would it put at risk personal files or online banking? Once malware is installed, the offender could potentially have full control of the device, including the camera and microphone, and access to contacts and saved passwords. The more the potential damage, the more security conscious you need to be. Whether on their own computer or on the family's, make sure your child follows the rules for cyber safety (see box, right) and back up anything important.

What should you do if it's already happened?

Don't think that if you pay up, it'll stop—it very rarely does. And don't assume that someone claiming to have compromising material actually does. Some would-be blackmailers and extorters are bluffing. Ask for evidence. If they can't provide it, they don't have it; if they do provide it, it's crucial evidence to take to the authorities. Criminals are generally lazy, especially online. If you're difficult, they'll usually give up and find an easier target.

If the problem is ransomware and your child's device is locked, again, don't pay up; giving your bank details to criminals is a bad idea. You may need to do a factory reset of the device (see p.209) or reinstall the operating system (get advice on how to do this from a computer support shop), and then restore your child's data from a backup. If their email account has been compromised, they need to create a new one, shut down the old one, and warn friends and family not to open any emails they receive from the old account.

It is important that your child feels able, and knows, to approach you if anything like this happens. There's no guarantee that it won't be temporarily embarrassing or that images won't be leaked to the public even if you do pay, but these things can be resolved.

When should you seek outside help?

Extortion, blackmail, and coercion are all very serious criminal offenses worldwide, and you need to report them to the police—not only for your child but also to prevent others from being targeted. Most extortionists, even the very sophisticated ones, will be caught.

Gather as much evidence as you can: screenshots of messages, along with date and time, records of usernames and the sites or services they're used on, and anything else that might be relevant. If the site has an abuse-reporting button, use it and provide as much detail as you can in your report.

If it's a revenge attack from somebody you or your child know, you could warn them before contacting the police. The prospect of a prison sentence may make them stop. If you're unsure who the perpetrator is, discuss possible suspects with your child. If appropriate, discreetly message each person separately, telling them that your child has been subject to an online threat (don't say what) and that you will contact the police if it isn't rescinded.

If the perpetrator does share intimate photos or information online, again, gather as much evidence as you can and also report the content to the site owner(s) (see pp.226–227).

GOLDEN RULES FOR CYBER SAFETY

Make sure your child follows these strict ground rules:

- Don't trust strangers on the Internet, no matter how nice they seem.

- Never send a picture you wouldn't want all your friends or family to see.

- Never download anything—whether it's music, a video, a GIF (a moving image), or a game—sent by a stranger.

- Never click on a link in a message or email unless you know the sender and know the sender's account hasn't been compromised.

- Never use sites that require webcams to participate.

- Don't click on a link or download button promising something valuable for free.

- Never pay a ransom, and never give in to demands of any kind. Don't believe they'll go away after one payment.

PARENTS' QUESTIONS ANSWERED

My son thought he was talking to another boy online and did "some things" on a webcam. Now it turns out there was no boy, and he's being blackmailed for money.

You need to know what you're dealing with before considering what to do. Ask your son a few questions, or if he is reluctant to talk to you, get another trusted adult to ask. First, try to ascertain what he did on the webcam. This can be difficult, but he needs to be honest—even though it may be embarrassing, it will be more embarrassing if it goes public. Ask him what kind of material the other person has: is it a video or pictures? Find out the site or service he used and whether he used his own webcam or someone else's, which could put them at risk, too.

Ask about the images: do they show his face, or is there anything that indicates where he lives or goes to school? Does the person know your son's first name or any personal details about his life or your family? Find out exactly what your son has told this person and whether he's been chatting with him on any other social media sites. Finally, what course of action is being threatened if your son doesn't pay up?

What can we do to stop them?

Many extortionists are lazy, so if your son ignores them, there's a very good chance they'll go away without delivering on threats. Check his privacy settings and unfriend or block anyone he doesn't know. However, if the other person has your son's personal details or starts threatening your son on his other social media accounts, report the messages to the

33%

of **SEXTORTION VICTIMS DON'T CONFIDE** in **ANYONE** about their situation because they feel **ASHAMED** or **EMBARRASSED** or **BLAME THEMSELVES.**

site(s) concerned. Most big-name social networks have solid reporting systems. Keep a note of any messages sent and of any contact you have with the networks' abuse-reporting teams. Contact the police if the extortion persists.

If your son thinks he knows who is behind it, you could approach them first and ask them to stop before you get the school involved or go to the police.

Are there ways to find out who this person is?

If it isn't somebody your son knows, that's best left to the police. You could employ an investigator, but if the situation's serious enough to consider such an expense, then it's important enough to consider getting the police involved.

What if the extortionist is in another country? Can the authorities here still help?

Yes, they can. The world is a smaller place than you might think, and law enforcement agencies work with their counterparts across the world. Your son could have been the target of an international cybercrime group; if so, there's a very good chance that his extortionist is already known to law enforcement somewhere. Other people may have reported them, and they could be the subject of an active investigation.

In the future, how can my son determine whether someone really is who they say they are?

It's difficult. He should never trust anybody unless he knows them in the real world. He should also think about the kinds of conversations he has online. Are they like the ones he has in real life? For example, people may be less inhibited online than they are in real life, but it's unlikely that if he met a girl or boy of the same age in a nonsexual forum that they'd demand intimate secrets or images in a matter of minutes— so if that happens online, it should set off red flags.

The question he also needs to consider constantly is: does this person sound like a normal boy or girl, or does this person sound like somebody older pretending to be a boy or girl?

In 2016, there were

1,250

reported cases of **SEXTORTION** in the UK. That's more than **DOUBLE** the number reported in 2015.

> **My son has installed something on the family computer that's encrypted everything—it says I can't unlock computer without paying money. HELP!**

This is called ransomware. It's likely that it snuck onto your system when your son clicked on a link in an email or message, or by being hidden in a movie, music, video, or game file he downloaded from a file-sharing site.

First of all, don't pay. There's no guarantee that your computer will be unlocked if you do, and it's quite likely that you'll just be asked to pay again. Even worse, if you give the criminals your bank card details, they can use them to run up huge debts or empty your bank account very quickly

Second, don't install anything the ransomers ask you to. They may want to install software to spy on everything you do, such as online banking, or even turn on your webcam.

If you're conned into handing over card details or account logins, many banks may not refund the money even if the perpetrators are caught and convicted.

Is there a way to remove ransomware from the system without losing all our files?

That depends on what particular form of ransomware you're dealing with. There are three types: scareware, lock-screen scareware, and serious ransomware. Both types of scareware can be fairly easily removed, but serious ransomware will encrypt and lock all the data on your computer, making it much more difficult to remedy.

Scareware is fake ransomware. It often pretends to be a legitimate antivirus program, but it blasts you with alerts and other pop-ups, often asking for money to sort them out. Even the simplest (legitimate!) antivirus software can detect and delete this kind of ransomware.

Every

4.2

SECONDS,
a **NEW**
malware **SCAM**
EMERGES on
the Internet.

Lock-screen scareware locks your computer and displays a notice, sometimes pretending to be from law enforcement or an organization such as the FBI. If you don't pay up, you can't unlock the computer. Again, this is a bluff: it's just something that loads when the computer starts up, and it's often simple for a computer repair shop to detect and resolve the download causing the issue.

And then there's the serious stuff. If a program scrambles your data, something called "encryption," then it may be impossible to decrypt that data without the correct "key"— a digital code without which your data is unreadable.

If you're not technically minded, you could try your local computer repair shop in the hope that it's a known problem that somebody is able to fix relatively easily. But if it's serious ransomware, in most cases the only way to get rid of this kind of malicious software is to completely reset your computer. If you don't have an up-to-date backup, that means you'll lose anything you've done since the last backup. If you've never backed up, you're going to lose everything on the computer.

If that prospect horrifies you, there are data recovery tools that might be able to access files—forensic experts use them to analyze criminals' computers and recover deleted files— but that's a specialist job that could cost a lot of money.

If there's no fix for the problem, you don't want to lose data, and you're willing to wait, you could put the computer aside for a while and keep checking online to see if somebody designs a program to kill the software.

Can this issue infect any of our other devices?

That depends on how it got onto your system in the first place: if it's from a link that's been clicked or a file that's been downloaded, it could potentially affect any other device that runs the same software, such as a smartphone. However, such software doesn't usually jump from one operating system to another—so a Windows PC problem won't affect an Android phone or Apple Mac. Apple devices are generally harder to

NADIA:
This happened to my sister. She got some ransomware that froze her whole computer. She hadn't backed up, so she lost all her data!

KAYE:
Will, how do you do a backup? Are memory sticks old hat these days?

WILL:
The two best ways to back up your devices are by using an external solid state hard drive (SSD) and/ or the cloud. If you have an external hard drive, encrypt it, back up your devices regularly, and keep the hard drive safe.

compromise, but no system is 100 percent secure. If all your devices are Apple, be careful about Automatic Sync to iCloud as devices sharing the same account can become infected.

My partner runs his own business, and there are lots of files he needs immediate access to on the computer; should we just pay up?

No. There's no guarantee that you'll get the files back, and you definitely won't see your money again.

How can I prevent my son from downloading ransomware again?

There's no way to eradicate the risk completely, but some simple steps can reduce the danger (see the boxes on pp.138 and 139). Also make sure your son is able to spot suspicious communications. One common way to spread ransomware is via official-looking emails; for example, people pretend to work for Microsoft or Apple technical support, tell you they've spotted a serious problem with your computer, and ask you to download a tech support program. Boom: your computer's compromised. The software's there to spy on you.

Another common trick is to send official- or urgent-looking emails from banks or other financial organizations urging you to solve some kind of account problem. The link in the email takes you to a convincing fake website, designed to either get your login details or get you to download malicious software.

Apply common sense: if you've phoned a helpline, you'll know how long it takes to get through. They barely manage to cope with that, never mind patrolling the Internet proactively solving problems. And if you've had a genuine bank account problem, you'll know that they tend to stop your cards and telephone or text you. If in doubt, phone the bank or organization using the details on their website or on the back of your card. Back up anything important and check your antivirus software. And remember, it's not just kids who can compromise the computer—so follow these guidelines, too!

KAYE:
All of this is making me shudder. My kids have a computer in their playroom that I never use. Should I be doing some sort of simple maintenance to make sure nothing suspicious is on there?

WILL:
You don't need to do anything too complicated, Kaye, just check the computer once a week. If there are any notices telling you about updates for your antivirus software or operating system, install them. These systems will pick up on and alert you to any problems early.

I hear about kids being coerced into dangerous activities by online entities or chain mails—if they don't do something, harm or bad luck will come to them or their loved ones. How can I ensure my daughter is protected?

Viral chain letters have been around for hundreds of years: if you don't send this on, your ears will fall off, or your parents will die, or some such nonsense. Unfortunately, the Internet makes it much easier for this stuff to spread, and when it's done well, it can be pretty convincing. There's the classic "send this to 20 people in the next hour or you'll have bad luck forever!" and the more recent "My friend works for the security services and says there's going to be a terrorist attack today! Forward this to everyone you know!" The common denominator is that there's something you need to do, and if you don't do it, there will be terrible consequences.

If your child receives something promising terrible consequences if they don't send it to 50 friends (or conversely, promising that Bill Gates will give them a dollar for every person they send it to), get them to Google the message's promise, subject, or threat to teach them how to check whether a message or email is really real and help them understand hoaxes, urban myths, and other fakery.

KAYE:
I feel bad for kids having to navigate through all of this. Even if you don't use apps or play games, so much life admin is done on the Internet now. We all make mistakes, and it's not about making them feel stupid, just letting them know there are bad guys out there they need to know about.

Who preys on kids this way? What are they trying to accomplish?

It's usually other kids with overactive imaginations trying to give each other a scare. Sometimes, though, spooky content, messages, or media come from marketing companies trying to promote a product such as a scary movie: it's called viral marketing, and it induces users and websites to pass on the content, thus rapidly increasing its exposure. Successful examples include *The Blair Witch Project*, a low-budget horror movie that made nearly $250 million, and *Cloverfield*, which made $178 million. Recently, I've seen more sinister viral content designed to spread hate and fear of particular groups, such as people from specific religions or cultures.

What should I tell my daughter about this stuff?

First, tell her not to share it: it might alarm more vulnerable children or make people afraid of things they needn't be afraid of. In extreme cases, such as where content has been deliberately created to cause fear or distress, sharing it might be illegal. Encourage your child generally to always check whether something's true before deciding whether to share it. In an era of fake news, this kind of critical thinking is going to be more and more important for them as they grow older.

HACKING PEOPLE is **EASIER** than **HACKING COMPUTERS**, so **CRIMINALS** often **TRICK** people into **REVEALING** their **LOGIN** details instead of using **MALWARE**.

TAKEAWAYS

1 NEVER GIVE IN TO DEMANDS Extortion is illegal. If someone is threatening to release private images or data unless your child pays them, you should report it to the police, cut off contact, and secure their device and other social media accounts.

2 DON'T ENGAGE WITH EXTORTIONISTS Many scams are bluffs. If an extortionist gets nowhere with your child, they may simply move on to an easier target.

3 THINK BEFORE YOU CLICK Warn your child about emails, freebies, links, or downloads that just don't look right. They should delete them immediately without opening them.

4 UPDATE THEIR SECURITY Remind your child to regularly run antivirus and malware detection software on their computer and downloads, to run a virus check on downloads before opening them, and keep the software up-to-date.

5 REPORT ALL EXTORTION OR BLACKMAIL The perpetrators are usually caught, even if they're operating in a different country.

6 ALWAYS BACK UP Make sure your kids regularly back up their devices. This reduces the impact of ransomware since they can reset the device and restore the last backup.

7 DON'T FORWARD CHAIN LETTERS Explain to your child that chain letters might scare or fool others, even if they're funny.

8 DON'T PANIC! If your child gets a message about a problem with one of their online accounts, tell them to go to the site directly (type the normal address into their web browser) instead of following the link.

9 DON'T SCREEN SHARE Tell your kids that legitimate help sites will never ask them to download screen-sharing software or use their webcam.

WANT MORE INFO? If this chapter didn't answer all your questions, try:

- Cyberstalking and Tracking, see pp.84–87
- Online Shopping, see pp.151–153
- Device Safety and Security, see pp.202–215

ONLINE SHOPPING

HOW TO PROTECT YOUR CHILD FROM FAKES, FRAUD, THEFT, AND SCAMS

WHAT YOU NEED TO KNOW

KAYE'S EXPERIENCE

I am blushing as I write this. When I first realized that my daughter was buying and selling clothes online, it didn't occur to me for a second that there was anything to be wary of. I was too busy congratulating myself on having raised such an independent and entrepreneurial child. And, yes, as a canny Scot, I was also delighted that she wasn't coming to me to buy her the latest designer hoodie. I watched as she wrapped up sneakers and jeans that were either too small or she hardly wore and sent them off to addresses all over the country; I would smile as yet another package arrived at our door and found its way into her wardrobe. Never once did it occur to me to inquire which websites she was visiting, what form of payment she was using, which account the money was going into, what personal information she was sharing, or what conversations she was having with the people she was trading with.

My default position is that there are a lot more good people in the world than bad, and the majority will conduct themselves in an honest manner, and I stand by that. But the online world is vast and offers a cloak of anonymity. For the small number of rotten apples out there, it is the ideal landscape.

By good fortune, my daughter hasn't had any problems, but I managed, conveniently, to forget that I myself have been caught out on more than one occasion. The vacuum cleaner, from a well-known auction site, was on sale at half the recommended retail price. I made the online payment, and no vacuum arrived— but two policemen did. Apparently, I'd been caught in a well-established scam. A couple of con artists had made themselves almost $1.5 million by advertising products that didn't exist. All were relatively low-value items, and most people opted not to pursue the matter because of the sheer hassle factor. Once bitten, twice gullible: I then decided to get myself a bargain on a pair of

MORE AND MORE COUNTERFEIT GOODS

are being sold online, and spotting fakes is becoming **MUCH HARDER.**

UGG boots. They arrived from China looking like they had been stitched together by someone wearing boxing gloves. In both instances, I was cautioned that I was lucky not to have had my identity stolen in the process. Have you figured out why I am blushing?

WILL'S EXPERT ANALYSIS

Where there's money, there's criminal activity. The amount of online frauds, cons, and scams is terrifying, and there are lots of traps for people trying to get free things they'd usually pay for. I've lost track of how many of my clients have contacted me when they or their child has bought or sold an item online that never turned up or that they never received the money for. I've also dealt with people targeted on online auction sites and through shopping apps, as in the case below.

How big is the problem?

As we increasingly use the Internet for shopping, the number of online frauds grows, taking advantage of the unmarked borders of the web. One of the fastest-growing problems is of reputable sites unwittingly selling fake wares. Counterfeit and pirated goods make up about 2.5 percent of global imports, with US, Italian, and French brands the hardest hit and many of the proceeds going to organized crime.

IDENTITY FRAUD is ON THE RISE. In 2017, there was an increase of **1 MILLION VICTIMS** in the US from the previous year.

WILL'S CASE STUDY

BOY CONNED OUT OF $250 AFTER BEING LURED OFF-SITE WITH THE PROMISE OF A DISCOUNT

A client's son had been on a "buy-sell" app to buy some jeans. The seller told him that he could have lots of other clothes at a great discount, too, but only if they communicated off the site. My client's son didn't have enough money for the bundle, so the seller said that he would accept tech instead.

The seller then came to my client's house and took her son's iPhone, iPad, and Mac but never handed over the bundle. My client was too frightened to tell the police because the seller knew where they lived.

KEY RISKS

Here are the most common scams your child may encounter when buying or selling online:

● **Identity theft** Your child's personal information and payment details are stolen.

● **Advance fee frauds** These are the too-good-to-be-true offers that promise big winnings. All your child needs to do is pay this fee first…

● **Phishing** Links in pages, emails, or messages offer something for free but actually link to sites where their data can be harvested or malicious software downloaded.

● **Pagejacking and pharming** When malicious software redirects your child to a fraudulent website.

● **Government warnings and tech-support scams** Usually presenting as intimidating notices on-screen, these are fake warnings of virus infections, illegal use, or even the FBI monitoring your PC.

● **Fake markets and products** Sites may be fake, or there may be fake sellers on legitimate sites. Products may be fake, have misleading descriptions, or simply not exist.

● **Stealth purchases** Sneaky add-ons or subscriptions your child didn't realize they signed up for.

Fakes are no longer bad knockoffs sold on market stalls. They're often very hard to distinguish from the real thing, whether clothes, makeup, or smartphone chargers. There's a growing problem of electrical items with unsafe chargers and laptop batteries that pose a fire hazard being sold on reputable shopping and auction sites.

Online frauds can run up huge bills with other people's card details; in 2016, 15.4 million consumers in the US alone were defrauded. Children are particularly vulnerable because they are less skeptical and more likely to be duped. Also, the sheer volume of products embedded in social media feeds means that they are constantly tempted to buy.

How could it affect your family?

Items that your child has purchased may not turn up or may bear no relation to what they're supposed to be. It may be difficult to get money back, and freebies may contain malicious software or fraudulent links (see box, left). It could even lead to theft (see p.151).

Online shopping can also be extremely addictive. The same "hit" we get from buying an item in person is obtained with far greater ease online, and the simple click to purchase makes it easy to ignore the impact on the wallet.

And as many adults can attest, bidding sites, such as eBay, can be particularly exciting. I've encountered several cases of children using their parents' credit card or PayPal account to make purchases or, worse, selling parents' items to make money.

How do you prevent it from happening?

Don't let your child use your bank cards, and don't set up "auto fill" for bank cards or financial services, such as PayPal, on any device your child has access to. If you want your child to have a junior account with a debit card, set up a prepaid debit card with set funds linked to an app where you can approve transactions. And never, ever, reuse the same passwords across different sites or services.

Make sure your child buys goods only from reputable sites. Never buy from a website if the padlock icon or "https" doesn't appear in the address bar of your web browser in the payment area of the site. The locked padlock and "s" mean it's secure; if these aren't there, don't use the site. Your child should also be aware of fake reviews: just because an item has 200 five-star reviews doesn't mean these are real or reliable. If in doubt, show your child how to Google the product for a range of reviews.

Warn your child not to give out unnecessary personal information and to never go outside the usual channels; on eBay, for example, if your child agrees to pay or accept payment privately, they lose all their buyer or seller protection and any rights they have within the website. They are also potentially putting themselves at great risk.

What should you do if it's already happened?

If a site has sent the wrong item, use its complaints and/or returns section. Check whether a site charges "restocking" fees for returns—these are often illegal if the product is faulty or mis-sold.

Ask your child whether they've been using your card or password. If they've been shopping without your permission, remove access to your card details on their device, and make sure they don't have access to your device(s). If you can't be sure, ask your card provider for a new card with a new number. If your child admits to only a few purchases but a lot of packages have been delivered, check the site to see if your child has mistakenly signed up for repeat purchases or for auto-renewals and cancel these.

If you think someone has any of your or your child's passwords, change them immediately, and if two-factor authentication (see p.205) is available on a device(s), switch it on. Also, be sure to regularly check your bank balance for unauthorized spending.

When should you seek outside help?

If you're in dispute with an online seller, you may need your credit card provider or payment provider to investigate on your behalf. Gather as much evidence as you can.

If a credit card number is compromised, for example, because your child ordered from a fraudulent site or clicked a suspicious link, cancel the card at once to protect yourself from recurring charges and from the risk of your card being cloned.

STAYING SAFE

A growing number of marketplace sites are aimed at young people to buy, sell, or swap clothes and goods. Make sure your child follows these tips:

• Use only trusted sites, and do the transaction on the site itself using a secure payment system, such as PayPal. If selling on a social media marketplace, make sure people can't click on your user profile.

• Never give out a personal email, phone number, real name, location, or age.

• Use only the site's messaging system or set up a dedicated email just for buying and selling.

• Always use tracking that requires signature on receipt when posting the item.

• Make sure that the product image doesn't reveal personal details in the background: pictures of the family, other items of value, or the front of the house.

• Don't agree to any partial payment or a payment other than money for the transaction.

• If at any time the conversation feels suspicious, stop all communication.

• If the buyer or seller wants to meet in real life, a parent or another trusted adult must accompany the child and meet only in a public place.

PARENTS' QUESTIONS ANSWERED

My son paid for an app that turned out to be fake. It wasn't that expensive, but it was a lot of money at his age. How does this happen?

Authentic-looking counterfeits of big-name apps are an ongoing issue. They are more likely to be a problem on Android phones and tablets rather than on Apple, which checks apps pretty thoroughly, so the appearance of fakes on its App Store is very rare.

HOW TO SPOT SUSPICIOUS APPS

There are many apps out there that could be fakes or even stealing data from your device. These are indicators that will help you spot fakes, but if in doubt, a quick Google search should reveal if one is a scam.

1 They are not available on Google or Apple app stores

2 There's no developer email or contact details

3 Typos in the app description

4 A small number of short, generic, and positive reviews all posted within a short period of time and from the same country

The app's page in shop

The app's review page

The best way to avoid fake apps is to read the small print, and check, for example, if the developer's name is listed correctly or if there is an error or an additional word. Read the reviews, too, though these can be misleading or faked.

KAYE:
How ironic that in this digital world where everything is super fast, you have to stop to take time to read the Terms and Conditions...

Can the fake app be used to access his personal details or our family's?

That depends on what the app is designed to do or what else is on the device that it could access. If it isn't designed to steal entire identities, it can still access a fair amount of information. Although Google Play apps tell you what data they need when they're installing, for example, hardly anyone reads that information. So the app may access and have the ability to share location information, contacts, photos, or details of other social media accounts.

WILL:
Absolutely! There's more than a little truth in the old saying "the devil is in the detail."

My daughter bought some items that are clearly fake through a well-known site. The reviews were all really positive—don't sites check this stuff?

Not always. Many online marketplaces simply provide the Internet equivalent of a market stall: what's sold is not their concern. The idea that likes or reviews keep sellers honest and highlight the best ones is naive. If I see 500 five-star reviews, I assume that they've been bought. There are dozens of online sites with thousands of bots writing fake reviews.

UP TO 15% of all online reviews are **FAKE**—some companies pay for fake reviews to sell their products.

Are some sites worse than others, and can she trust a small, independent seller?

Marketplaces are where the real problems occur, but any high-profile site that enables other people to sell through it is

AVOIDING THE FAKES

Some sellers are frauds, trying to trick people into buying fake or broken products. Here are some of the ways to spot a suspicious seller:

1 Images don't show the laptop turned on; this could mean there is an issue with the screen, or it doesn't work at all

2 Spelling mistakes in product name and description

3 Discount is suspiciously high or the price is very low

4 Shipping and handling costs are excessively high

5 No way of contacting the seller

6 A small number of short, generic reviews all posted within a short period of time

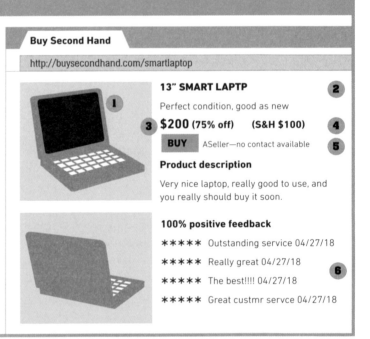

Buy Second Hand

http://buysecondhand.com/smartlaptop

13" SMART LAPTP 2

Perfect condition, good as new

3 **$200** (75% off)   (S&H $100) 4

BUY   ASeller—no contact available 5

Product description

Very nice laptop, really good to use, and you really should buy it soon.

100% positive feedback

★★★★★ Outstanding service 04/27/18

★★★★★ Really great 04/27/18

★★★★★ The best!!!! 04/27/18   6

★★★★★ Great custmr servce 04/27/18

CHECK FOR THE PADLOCK SIGN

and **SHOP ONLY ON SITES** where a **LOCKED PADLOCK SYMBOL** (or "https") is seen at the beginning of the web address during checkout and payment.

going to attract fakes and frauds. That doesn't mean your daughter shouldn't trust independent sellers—most of them are small businesses using the Internet to reach as many buyers as possible—but she should make sure she is dealing with reputable ones by doing a bit of checking. How long have they been selling online? What else do they sell? What do the negative and middling reviews or auction feedback ratings, if there are any, say about them? Do they provide any signs of being legitimate, such as which country they're located in, a company website, and, especially, contact details. Is there "https" at the beginning of the web address?

How can she tell if the picture of an item is accurate?

She should search for the product online to compare. It's highly unlikely that one website or individual will be the only one in the world selling it. If it's got a generic name, search the Internet for the image of the product.

With auctions and classifieds, photos can mislead: for example, if a laptop is being shown from every angle but never with the laptop switched on, that's often because it doesn't work or because maybe there's something wrong with the screen. Be cynical: is there something here you should be able to see but can't?

What comeback does my daughter have? Can she get a refund?

On well-known, reputable sites, there's a good chance she can get a refund, even if the seller is independent. It's more difficult on auction sites: carefully worded descriptions can mean that the buyer has no comeback. My favorite example is the boy who thought he was buying a boxed PlayStation game console based on the extensive photos of the console, its controllers, even the power supply, along with lots of blurb about the power of the PlayStation. But the listing title very clearly said, "Sony PlayStation brand new box," and that's what he got: an empty cardboard box that cost almost $300. Despicable? Absolutely. But not refundable.

There is a slight possibility your daughter may get her money back if she reports the seller to the site. This is because some sites hang on to sellers' money for a period of time in case of fraud. If nothing else, it will alert them to the presence of a suspicious seller so that they can ban them and prevent others from falling for the same scam.

If this is a counterfeit crime, should we report it to the police?

Reporting online scams to the police is unlikely to help you get your money back, but it may prevent others from being conned in the future. You can also contact consumer protection organizations, such as the Better Business Bureau or the FTC's Bureau of Consumer Protection (see p.232).

My credit card's been cloned, and I think it's because I let my daughter buy some stuff online with it. How easy is it for this to happen?

Criminals have been exploiting and hacking credit cards for years and are pretty good at it. With some basic card information, they can guess most security codes and expiration dates in under six seconds.

How could it have been cloned in the first place?

There are lots of ways. It could have been used on a website with poor security—no padlock or "https" in the browser's address bar—or from clicking a "phishing" link (see p.162) in an email or website, which takes you to a fake site that asks for your details. Or a reputable site could have been hacked and its customer database accessed. If you've used the same email and password combination elsewhere, the criminals have the key to your identity on multiple sites and services.

What can I do to protect my cards?

Use reputable websites, and never put your credit card details into a site you're not sure about. If you're using a third-party payment system, such as PayPal, set up an incredibly strong password and turn on PayPal Security Key, a form of two-factor authentication (see p.205) that sends a one-off code to your phone whenever you (or anybody else) tries to log in to your account with the correct username and password. And don't give your child unauthorized access to your card.

It's worth searching for your email address on a site called haveibeenpwned.com. This is a database of retailers that have been hacked. Searching your email address in its database may tell you if you've visited hacked retailers. If your email is listed, you should change your passwords immediately.

KAYE:
The blood is draining from my face here—ridiculously, my kids' thumbprints work on my phone, but mine doesn't, so they can access my cash. They haven't abused this, but I need to get a grip!

Why were all the false purchases made in really low amounts? Is this something to look out for?

Small purchases often fly below the radar: most people skim their statements and are happy if the balance looks about right. However, those tiny transactions can add up over time.

Small purchases could also be a red flag that the criminals are testing that the card details work before setting in motion a bigger scam, so it's vital to check statements thoroughly.

My daughter makes purchases with her smartphone and tablet away from home; is it more risky to shop from a public Wi-Fi than from home?

Yes. It's easy to intercept Wi-Fi signals and to set up fake but convincing Wi-Fi access points. If you're making a financial transaction on a network you don't own or trust, such as in a café, it's unsafe unless you use a VPN (virtual private network, see above) or a device's 2G, 3G, or 4G connection.

25%
of **PUBLIC WI-FI** networks have **NO ENCRYPTION** or **PASSWORD** protection of any kind.

I allowed my son to buy a game, but it's constantly demanding he spends money on silly additions. He's really pestering me. Surely games and apps aren't allowed to do that?

Many apps and games have in-app purchases. They're particularly common in free games—the idea is that you try the game for free and like it so much that you'll pay to unlock extra content. These are often offered in a drip-drip-drip way to keep milking customers for money.

There's nothing wrong with in-app purchases if they're upfront and honest; "try before you buy" has been around for hundreds of years. Where they're a problem is when they are designed specifically to squeeze money out of children. For

KAYE:
Part of the problem is that young people are dealing with "virtual" money. I recently interviewed a mom whose son ran up a bill of more than $500 because he kept being offered more Wi-Fi access and kept clicking, not realizing it was costing money.

example, there was a Smurfs game that sold baskets of berries you could use to decorate the Smurfs' village. One child ran up a bill of $1,400 before their parents realized.

Should I be worried that he might be able to spend money without me knowing?

Yes. It's essential that you control any bank card that's used for any app store or gaming service and that the app requests authorization before making purchases (see below). Your son should have to come to you for every in-app purchase.

As my credit card details are on file, how can I keep my card safe from future in-app purchases?

In most cases, the game or service will still need confirmation; for example, you can set your Apple ID to require a password or fingerprint for any downloads or purchases.

For online shopping sites, bank card details are usually stored without the three-digit security code. The checkout will ask for those details before confirming the purchase. To be extra safe, you could set up two-factor authentication (see p.205) for the account if it is available on that site.

It's also important to watch out for repeat payments, where the seller is permitted to bill you again and again.

85%
of the
$37 BILLION GLOBAL APP MARKET
is from games.

An offer for free makeup came to my daughter's email inbox from what looked like a popular beauty brand, and she clicked on it. Now she's signed up for a "free trial offer" that she actually had to pay for.

We can all fall prey to the "best deal" ever and end up on auto-renewable subscriptions without even realizing. The key message to communicate to your child is that nothing is ever really free. Sometimes a purchase may include a couple of extra items for free, but "free trials" are rarely so. Often these ask for credit card or online payment details to qualify then start charging after the first month, so you have to remember to cancel before this. Check the terms and conditions to see if this is how they operate. Make sure, too, that you control the payment details so that if your daughter wants something, she needs to come to you first. Online payment services, such as PayPal, are easier to cancel repeat payments from than credit cards. Check your credit card/online payment statements carefully. Many services take only a small monthly amount, which you might not notice until several months later.

Offers can also be "phishing" scams (see p.162), when what appears to be a legitimate site contains a link to a fake site. If you pass on your credit card or bank details, or even just your username or password, these can be exploited.

How are phishing sites set up, can we spot them, and what should we do if we click on one?

The Internet keeps a record of all your online activity. This is recorded by aggregators—people and organizations who collect all the related data of visits to websites, known as cookies. They sell this data to organizations who use clever algorithms to see what you like then email offers or post them on the sidebars of websites.

However, phishers will also send you fake warnings or offers that direct you to scam websites, a process known as "pagejacking." You are then enticed to register for services or buy products, or they may even load snooping spyware or viruses onto your device. One way to check if a website is real is to look in the browser address bar: does it have "https" at the beginning? If it is only "http" and doesn't have the "s" or a padlock symbol, it's unsecure, and you should close it. If you can't close it, you may have been pagejacked. Close your browser (or even restart your device completely) to get rid of it. When you have gotten rid of the page, run antivirus software to make sure it hasn't left anything nasty on your device.

Beware of **PHISHING SITES** impersonating tech companies. The sites last an average of only 15 hours, but **HUNDREDS OF THOUSANDS** of them appear every month.

PHISHING EMAILS AND LINKS

can look **EXTREMELY CONVINCING**—check sites carefully for subtle mistakes.

Are there other phishing tricks to look out for?

Phishers can pose as all sorts of organizations: the police, tax authorities, your favorite online store, and even charities and emergency relief funds. If, for example, a charity site looks odd (it might have typos in the address or website text), then open a new tab and Google the charity website to ensure that you are on the legitimate site.

Names can also be harvested from other websites you have visited. If you donated to a genuine charity or fundraiser or registered your email address with them, there might have been a box next to their Terms and Conditions asking if you would like to receive related information. If you ticked this, they can sell your details, and your email inbox could be swamped with worthy requests for donations.

Be aware that phishing messages aren't always emails; they could appear as pop-ups on suspicious websites, sent as text messages to your child's phone, or even be voice calls.

CATCHING A PHISHING EMAIL

Phishing emails may take the form of a special offer or an urgent warning about an online account. These are some telltale signs to help your child spot them:

1 The message is usually urgent or potentially worrying

2 Senders' email address doesn't match name of the bank or site

3 Names of other people sent the message are visible

4 Spelling and grammar mistakes

5 Hovering over the link reveals web address for the wrong site

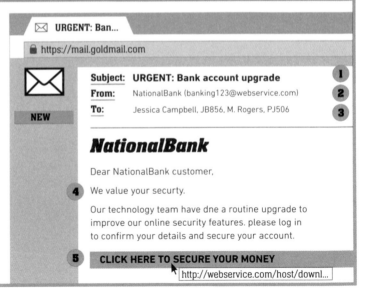

TAKEAWAYS

1 ALWAYS CHECK BEFORE GIVING AWAY PERSONAL DETAILS Online fraud can be financially crippling, so your child shouldn't hand over details unless they're 100 percent sure that a site is legitimate.

2 CONTROL PAYMENTS Make sure your child has to come to you to pay for an item, and avoid payment auto fills or one-click shopping.

3 LOOK OUT FOR THE PADLOCK OR "HTTPS" Make sure your child uses only sites where the padlock icon or "https" appears in the address bar of the browser when they make a payment, and pays only through the regulated site.

4 DON'T GO OFF-SITE Tell your child to never take a sale outside a legitimate website if the seller suggests a direct sale—they will lose all the protection the site offers.

5 ASK QUESTIONS If your child isn't sure if something is legitimate, contact the seller. Is the seller easy to contact and helpful?

6 READ THE REVIEWS A long list of five-star reviews should raise suspicions.

7 BE AWARE OF SCAMS Your child should never click on a link unless it's from a trusted source. If a link has been sent to them, they should be suspicious.

8 DON'T BE FOOLED BY FAKES Your child should be on the alert for counterfeit goods, fake sites, fake sellers, fake reviews—and even fake charity "causes."

9 BE ARMED AGAINST MANIPULATION Alert your child to the psychological tricks criminals will use to convince them to trust a link, seller, or site.

WANT MORE INFO? If this chapter didn't answer all your questions, try:

- Device Safety and Security, pp.200–217
- Buying Illegal Products, pp.167–169, pp.222–225
- Social Engineering, p.103

COSMETICS, DRUGS, AND LEGAL HIGHS

THE EASY AVAILABILITY OF DANGEROUS AND UNREGULATED SUBSTANCES

WHAT YOU NEED TO KNOW

NADIA'S PERSPECTIVE

The fact that medicines and legal highs are so readily available online is a great worry to me. I had serious body issues when I was growing up, believing, like many young girls, that I was fat (I was not!). It caused me enough anguish that if slimming pills had been available online, believe you me, I would have taken them by the bucket load. We all know the devastating physical and psychological damage that such pills can cause!

I worry that my girls are even more vulnerable to having body issues than I was as a teenager. I know this may be partly due to my influence, but they also face an enormous amount of pressure from the constant barrage of "perfect" images they have to swipe past on all the social media platforms.

I also worry about the peer pressure my girls will face to experiment with legal highs. I can just hear the other kids already saying, "Come on, it's legal; it can't do you any harm; everyone is doing it!" As a bit of a wild child myself, I could have easily gotten into trouble with this kind of persuasion. I have a dear friend whose son was convinced by a group of friends in his college dorm that the drug "spice" (which was legal at the time) was perfectly safe. Needless to say, it all ended very badly when he had to be admitted to the hospital. Thankfully, he lived to tell the tale, but, as he very well knows, this really was down to luck; stories abound of students overdosing on various kinds of legally bought drugs.

What's more, these days you don't even have build up the courage to meet drug dealers to buy drugs; you can just order them online, and they'll arrive in the mail. Truly startling.

My husband and I regularly have discussions with both of our girls about the perils and dangers of drugs online—we would prefer to be their primary source of information rather than other kids!

WILL'S EXPERT ANALYSIS

With the freedom the Internet provides, the process of buying medicines and drugs online is frighteningly easy. Pharmaceuticals that require a prescription from a doctor in your country can be bought from foreign countries where different restrictions apply and sent directly to your door. These drugs can be dangerous in the wrong quantities, or they may be counterfeit, or, if they interact with food or other medications, can cause serious side effects or even death.

Children are often most vulnerable—birth control, body image, or an embarrassing condition are all things teens might not want to speak to a parent or a doctor about. The Internet seems to provide a way to self-diagnose, self-prescribe, and self-treat, as shown below.

Other concerns are legal highs, mind-altering substances either not intended for human consumption or designed to get around the law; "smart" drugs used to improve concentration and memory; unregulated cosmetic treatments and diet pills, which often contain banned substances; and unlicensed steroids. These products can do serious damage to people's bodies.

In 2015, Interpol's Operation Pangea seized more than

20 MILLION

counterfeit or illicit pills from **2,410 WEBSITES** in 115 **COUNTRIES.**

How big is the problem?

Counterfeit and synthetic medicine is a huge problem online. Many pills that are seized by law enforcement could have caused

SHOCK DISCOVERY OF TEENAGE BOY'S DANGEROUS STEROID ABUSE

A client came to me with concerns about her 14-year-old son's behavior. He had been spending a lot of time working out, complaining that his friends were more muscly and that this attracted girls. He had become increasingly obsessive, not only exercising excessively but also watching endless videos on bodybuilding.

I advised her to check his room for any signs of performance-enhancing drug use, and she was shocked when she stumbled across several hypodermic needles under his bed. She also found a number of vials of anabolic steroids, which carry serious health risks. She couldn't bear to think about what could have happened if he'd continued.

KAYE:
This wasn't even on my radar. Even if I was worried about my daughter's behavior, I wouldn't think she was buying drugs online. How common is this, Will?

WILL:
Stats are hard to find, but teen drug use is on the rise. In 2017, one in four children aged 11–15 said they had tried cannabis, cocaine, or legal highs.

WHAT'S OUT THERE?

Teen online purchases may include:

- Prescription medicines
- "Smart" drugs
- Birth control pills
- Hormone supplements
- Weight-loss pills
- Anabolic steroids/muscle enhancers
- Testosterone boosters
- Cosmetic fillers
- Skin creams
- Teeth-whitening products
- Legal highs
- Illegal recreational drugs

serious damage or even killed somebody if taken inappropriately. Fake drugs and man-made "highs" can come from anywhere, and they're shipped worldwide. Many are sold on major, trusted platforms or by online pharmacies, so you don't even have to go to the "dark" web to find them. (The dark web is part of the Internet where sites sell illegal products, such as drugs, guns, or stolen identities, and offer information on how to commit crimes. It is where some of the most horrible things happen online.) Drugs can also be found on social media sites and even on messaging apps.

How could it affect your family?

Your child may receive pills containing the wrong quantities of the ordered drug, or even dangerous substances instead. Unregulated pharmaceuticals can lead to serious illness, long-term health problems, and even death. And that's assuming that your child has self-diagnosed correctly—even if they received the right drug, it may not be appropriate for the condition they're trying to self-treat.

There's also the risk that other family members, such as younger siblings, might take the drug by mistake or out of curiosity. I've dealt with several cases where a child hid medication bought online in places where their younger siblings could easily have discovered them, or in a container labeled as containing a legitimate drug.

How do you prevent it from happening?

Keep an eye on your child—do they appear very body conscious or depressed? If your child reveals a problem, be supportive and suggest going to a doctor. If your child wants to buy medication online, help them to understand that there's rarely such a thing as safe medicine bought on the Internet. Although to them it may seem like a cheaper, more convenient, and less embarrassing way to treat a problem, explain that the dangers far outweigh the benefits, so it's not worth risking their health. It may also be illegal.

It's important that older children who might want to experiment with so-called legal highs realize that "legal" doesn't mean safe. Memory-enhancing "smart" drugs aren't safe, either; these can have unpleasant side effects, even if used as recommended. And there is no data that proves they are safe to use long term. In reality, you can try your best to dissuade your child, but they may still take these drugs regardless. If this is the case, try to guide them as best as you can (see right), and make sure they don't have access to your credit card, bank account, or PayPal details.

What should you do if it's already happened?

If you stumble across medication or drugs, ask your child why they have them. Talk to them about their concerns; be as supportive as you can, and don't exclude the possibility of legitimate medical solutions. Take the product to a pharmacy to be destroyed, and, if required, take your child to a doctor to get supervised treatment.

You'll also need to find out how your child got hold of the drugs: did they buy them themselves or through a friend? If it's the latter, you'll need to speak to the other child's parents. If your child bought them, they've probably used your credit card or PayPal or paid by bank transfer. Check your statements to find the payments and see if this is a one-off or a regular occurrence, and make sure they don't have any further access to your payment details.

When should you seek outside help?

If your child is suffering any kind of side effect, you need to get them professional medical care—at the hospital if you think it's urgent, or see your doctor if not. Bring the medication or drugs that they've been taking with you to help the experts diagnose the problem and identify the right treatment.

If you suspect that your child is passing on the medication or pharmaceuticals to somebody else, keep an open mind about whether they have done so willingly—an agreement between friends may have escalated beyond their control, or they may be acting under pressure from a peer group. If it's the latter, you may need to contact the other child(ren)'s parents, the school, or even the police, because inciting someone to commit a crime is a criminal offense. It's worth telling your child the legal risks associated with supplying other people with illegal or prescription drugs—a criminal record that will stay with them for the rest of their life.

GUIDING YOUR CHILD

If your child has medical concerns, always encourage them to consult a doctor. Teach your child how dangerous these sites are, using the questions below, and stress that there are no guaranteed safe ways to buy drugs online:

- Is the site offering prescription drugs without needing a prescription? This means your child's medical history won't be taken into account, with potentially dangerous results.

- Does the site overpromise? Does it say a medicine will cure a long list of varied conditions?

- Does the site say that the drug can be purchased only for a limited period of time?

- Is it clear who runs the website? Is there an address or telephone number?

- If the website contains advertisements, are they separated from the information about the products the website is selling?

PARENTS' QUESTIONS ANSWERED

My son is into bodybuilding, and I worry that he might try to get steroids or other performance-enhancing drugs over the Internet. Am I right to be concerned?

Possibly, yes. Boys can have body image issues, too, and he may be comparing himself to photographs of people who are older and more developed or who'll risk their health to look more muscular. There's no such thing as a get-fit-quick shortcut, but for somebody who's in a hurry to bulk up, there are plenty of people offering miracle solutions and supposed "body hacks"—drinks or pills that get visible results more quickly than healthy eating and exercise.

Try to steer him toward professionals, such as qualified fitness trainers at the local gym, or credible role models, such as athletes who talk about the risks of taking supplements. Steroids are known to cause emotional mood swings, from "roid rage" to depression in some young men. There is also the risk that the steroids he receives are fakes.

Other drugs that your son might turn to include human growth hormone (used alongside anabolic steroids to boost muscle growth) and synthol (a muscle filler). Even in relatively small amounts, human growth hormone can potentially cause bloating, gynecomastia ("man boobs"), and pain in the wrists and hands; larger doses risk mental illness, diabetes, and painfully enlarged hands and feet.

Synthol is the name used for a variety of oils that can be injected into the muscles to make them bigger. It is used in moderation by some professional bodybuilders but has

Children as young as

13

are using **ANABOLIC STEROIDS.**

become something of a fad for amateurs to get an immediate, pumped-up look. However, the process can lead to a host of problems, including nerve damage and a loss of blood flow to the muscles, and if he uses shared or unsterilized needles, he is running the risk of contracting an infection, such as hepatitis or HIV. Synthol also does nothing to make muscles stronger.

What's social media's role in all of this?

Surfing through photo-based social media, such as Instagram, you'll see enough men and women showing off their finely honed physiques to make already self-conscious teens feel thoroughly inadequate. Children don't think of the skilled Photoshop user removing the imperfections, even with those "before" and "after" photos. When it comes to bodybuilders, those biceps may be the work of endless gym sessions—or they could be synthol. It's crucial our children understand that what you see online isn't always real. There are no shortcuts to real fitness.

NADIA:
This applies to other areas, too, not just bodybuilding. On a weekly basis, I have to convince my youngest that all the "wonder" cosmetics she sees on Instagram can't possibly deliver on those ludicrous promises.

How will I know if he's bought and/or is stockpiling steroids?

The most obvious signs are overdevelopment and sudden muscle gain. Has he become visibly bigger (especially in the arms, chest, and leg muscles) despite sticking to the same gym routine and diet? These changes are obvious and can appear quickly, in some cases in around a month. There's often visible acne, most commonly on the face or back. Other signs may include agitation, aggression, depression, and insomnia.

How dangerous can steroids be?

Very. In addition to the risks attached to using unsterilized needles, possible side effects of steroid use include vomiting blood, acne, nausea, baldness, insomnia, abdominal pain, high cholesterol, blood clots, increased cancer risk, and potential liver damage. Abusing steroids can also stunt adolescent growth and may age bones prematurely.

More than

50%

of anabolic steroid users cited **DEVELOPMENT OF BODY IMAGE** as a key motivator for using the drug. Just 25% mentioned a desire for better athletic performance.

There are also long-term risks to mental health, and there is a strong correlation between steroid use and violent crime, including domestic violence. Anabolic steroids affect your hormones, which are incredibly powerful chemicals, and can even cause infertility. Taking steroids at any time is incredibly risky, but it's even riskier when you're under 20, because your hormones are still making big changes to your body.

Are these substances illegal?

That depends on where you live. In some countries, substances such as steroids and human growth hormone are classified alongside tranquilizers—that means it's illegal to sell them to somebody who doesn't have a prescription, but it isn't illegal to buy them or possess them provided it's for personal use. Synthol is perfectly legal and widely available. However, as with legal highs, "legal" doesn't mean "safe."

I've got a hypochondriac for a child; he's always looking up various ailments online and using symptom checkers. Is he getting accurate information and advice?

Millions of people self-diagnose on the Internet: in the US, one in three adults seeks medical advice online every day. There's a bleak joke that whatever symptoms you Google, you'll always discover that you have cancer. While that might not be entirely accurate, what is true is that if you search for a bunch of symptoms, you'll generally end up with bad advice, conspiracy theories, and unfounded diagnoses.

Online symptom checkers run by reputable organizations provide a slightly better option. In the first wide-scale review of general purpose symptom checkers (carried out by researchers at Harvard Medical School), these checkers were found to be roughly as reliable as the telephone triage helplines commonly used in primary care practice. The 23 symptom checkers studied provided the correct practical advice in 58 percent of nonurgent cases (although that still means 42 percent of nonurgent cases get the wrong advice). This makes them better than blind Internet searches but still no substitute for a professional medical consultation.

Is self-diagnosing something I should discourage? Will any harm come from it?

There's a reason medical staff have to study for so many years. Diagnosing a condition isn't just about ticking boxes; it's also about understanding the nuances and relevant factors—you need to know that symptoms for one disease might actually also be a sign of an entirely different condition.

Lupus, for example, is an autoimmune disease that affects millions of people, but doctors often misdiagnose it because it resembles many similar but different conditions that need different treatments. If the doctors struggle, what chance does an ordinary person or a computer algorithm have of getting it right?

There are two dangers with self-diagnosis. First, your child might misdiagnose themselves and think that something that is serious isn't and decide not to seek treatment. Second, your child may take the wrong medication or take a substance that interferes with existing medication. Drugs and herbal remedies can interact in unpleasant ways. For example, the herb St. John's wort, often recommended for depression, can be dangerous when taken alongside some prescription drugs.

Doctors need to consider all these factors. That's a level of knowledge and experience that goes way beyond being able to Google your symptoms and read a couple of studies.

Almost **40%** of general online symptom searches provide the **WRONG ADVICE** for urgent cases.

ILLEGAL PRESCRIPTION SITES

frequently shut down to **EVADE DETECTION**, only to reopen under a different name.

Do some sites offer medical advice just to get you to buy products from them?

Yes, so be very wary of any supposed medical advice where there's a shopping service attached. Not all such information is bad, but a lot of it is—especially on sites selling dubious or dangerous products. For example, I've seen sites selling diet pills containing the banned chemical DNP, which is known to have caused several deaths.

What about symptom checkers that aren't obviously selling something?

They may be selling something indirectly. If they link to sites that sell products, or mention specific product names, they may be getting paid to do so. Some are "affiliate links"—when you click them, the site you go to records the click, records who sent you to the page, and gives them a small cut of the sale. Some sites ask you to fill out a questionnaire before giving results, and then pass this data on to an affiliate.

My daughter has bought some strong acne medication from an online pharmacy. They gave her an "online consultation." Is this advice reliable?

No, these questionnaires are simply box-ticking exercises designed to try to prevent the online shop from being sued or to sell her details on. A real doctor will take all the key factors into consideration before prescribing anything—not only age, height, and build but also allergies, medical history, diet, any other medications being taken, and anything else that might affect the substance that is being prescribed.

Does this process make it easy for my daughter to lie about her age or condition?

Yes, sometimes the age verification is simply a box you tick to say, "I'm over 18." If you can access a credit card, you can usually buy the product.

How do we know if the seller is legitimate?

You don't, although willingness to sell prescription medicines without a prescription is a pretty big hint that they're not. Just because a website looks professional doesn't mean it's reputable or based where it appears to be. For example, many online pharmacies supposedly from the UK or US are actually based in Hong Kong or registered to shell companies there who sell products from labs in China.

KAYE:
Will, are any of these sites subject to any regulation at all? Are there any that are safe?!

WILL:
Very rarely, Kaye. Most site are based in China, India, or other markets that aren't stringently regulated.

Can we tell from the packaging if it's not the real deal?

Not necessarily. Sometimes the fakes are made in the same place as the real stuff, or very close by, and that means they can be sent in legitimate packaging. Even security holograms don't guarantee that what you see is what it claims to be.

What recourse do we have if she has a reaction to the medicine or needs aftercare?

If your daughter has a reaction to the medicine, seek professional medical help. However, there's no action you can take against the site (even to get your money back). That's why there is a system of doctors and prescriptions, so there is someone responsible for ensuring we get the right drug and dosage and that we don't suffer serious side effects. If you bypass that system, you lose all the protection and safeguards. If you or your daughter are

As many as
85%
of sites selling medicinal drugs **DON'T ASK FOR A DOCTOR'S PRESCRIPTION** or even proof of age.

concerned about her acne, the best thing you can do is go to a registered pharmacist, dermatologist, or doctor about it. Online pharmacies might look respectable, but looks can be deceiving.

> **I found some stuff in my son's coat that I thought was drugs, but he says it's a legal high. I've checked, and he's telling the truth. Does that mean it's safe?**

No. Just because something is legal to buy doesn't mean it is safe to consume. Often something being a legal high simply means that it isn't illegal yet.

So legal highs don't stay legal forever?

That's right. This is a fast-moving area, so in many countries, the more notorious legal highs are no longer legal. Some legal highs could easily end up being classed alongside the most serious illegal narcotics, and if that happens, then possessing those substances, or distributing them, could become just as bad as possessing or selling class-A drugs, such as heroin or cocaine.

What kind of things are legal highs made from?

There are two kinds of legal highs. The first kind are existing legal substances that are being misused. These are generally labeled unsafe for human consumption and sold as salts, incense, plant food, and even pond cleaner by sites that are well aware of what their customers are really buying them for. This category includes household items, such as solvents, which many people use to get a high; they, too, can have serious effects.

KAYE:
Just how easy are these for children to get hold of online, Will? Are there sites set up for this sole purpose—to sell these household products for use as drugs?

WILL:
Some are, but many are even less sophisticated. For example, do an Internet search for "cannabis + Adderall," and a surprising number of hits will come up.

The second (and much more frightening) kind of legal highs are synthetic drugs designed specifically to get around existing laws and/or make existing drugs much more powerful. For example, synthetic cannabinoids, such as "spice," are a mix of plant material and man-made chemicals designed to be a super-charged version of cannabis. These new drugs have been dubbed "zombie drugs" for their debilitating effects.

Is there such a thing as a safe dose?

No. How do you know what's safe if you don't know how much of the drug a pill contains or what other substances might have been added to it? If your child overdoses, medical staff may have no idea what substance they are actually trying to counteract.

We don't know about long-term exposure, either, as most legal highs are less than five years old. However, we do know that many of them contain chemicals with proven links to cancer, dementia, and liver and kidney disease. Studies also suggest that long-term use of legal highs may result in a range of mental health problems, such as anxiety, depression, and memory loss.

My son's behavior has changed, and I suspect he's taking illegal drugs. I've heard about online supermarkets for illegal drugs on the dark web. How do I know if he is accessing these sites or buying from them?

The dark web refers to websites that exist on an encrypted network—sites you can't access via Google. Instead, he would need to have installed an anonymity program, such as Tor, which hides online activity. If you suspect that he's buying

ACCESSING THE DARK WEB

Accessing the dark web requires the use of programs such as Tor, which allow Internet users to browse online anonymously.

Tor is not just used to access the dark web. It is useful for journalists protecting sources, those in oppressive regimes, etc. But if your child has downloaded Tor, you seriously need to ask them why. If it's to hide their identity, a good VPN will do this (see p.203).

Your Internet service provider can see any encrypted data leaving your computer, so they could associate it with a specific device. As the bill payer, you could be held responsible for your child visiting any illegal sites.

1 The connection enters the Tor network.

2 It is relayed through thousands of other users in the network and encrypted at each one.

3 The connection leaves the Tor network and goes to the desired website.

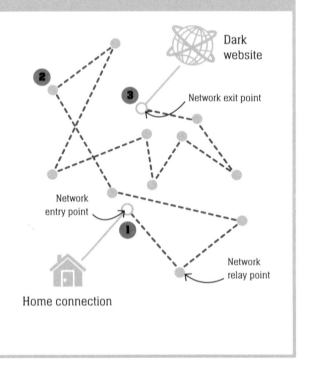

Dark website

Network exit point

Network entry point

Network relay point

Home connection

drugs online, these could be from the dark web. Illegal drug selling on the regular Internet tends to get picked up quickly, so dealers prefer the relative safety of the dark web. Is there software you don't recognize on his computer? Or have you noticed unexplained transactions to a software company on your bank statement?

What are the risks of buying drugs online?

As with taking any unknown drug, he risks his long-term health, an overdose, or even death. There are legal risks, too. Sellers may actually be law enforcement carrying out sting operations, and if he buys large amounts, he can be charged with intent to supply. Finally, payment methods can be cloned, or it could be a scam.

TAKEAWAYS

1 BE AWARE OF THE LACK OF REGULATION Age checks for medicines are often lax, or nonexistent, so children can buy potentially dangerous products with just a credit card.

2 DON'T ALLOW ACCESS TO YOUR PAYMENT METHODS Make sure your child has to come to you before making any online purchase.

3 DON'T SELF-DIAGNOSE Talk to your child about how unreliable online medical information can be and how only real-life doctors can give accurate assessments. Explain that there are no miracle cures.

4 CONSULT A DOCTOR Don't dismiss your child's worries about their health or appearance, but encourage them to see a doctor or counselor to talk through concerns.

5 EXPLAIN THE RISKS Talk about how dangerous substances are unlikely to be flagged up and that they shouldn't expect to have rights when it comes to returning drugs or medication or expect to be reimbursed for fakes.

6 LOOK OUT FOR WARNING SIGNS Watch for behavioral and physical changes in your child and investigate the reasons behind these.

7 DESTROY ONLINE DRUGS Explain that these could have health and legal repercussions; ask gently why they got them—keep an open mind.

8 LEGAL DOESN'T MEAN SAFE Your child may have no idea what's in legal highs, or what effect they may have. Also, that legal high may not be legal for long.

WANT MORE INFO? If this chapter hasn't answered all your questions, try:

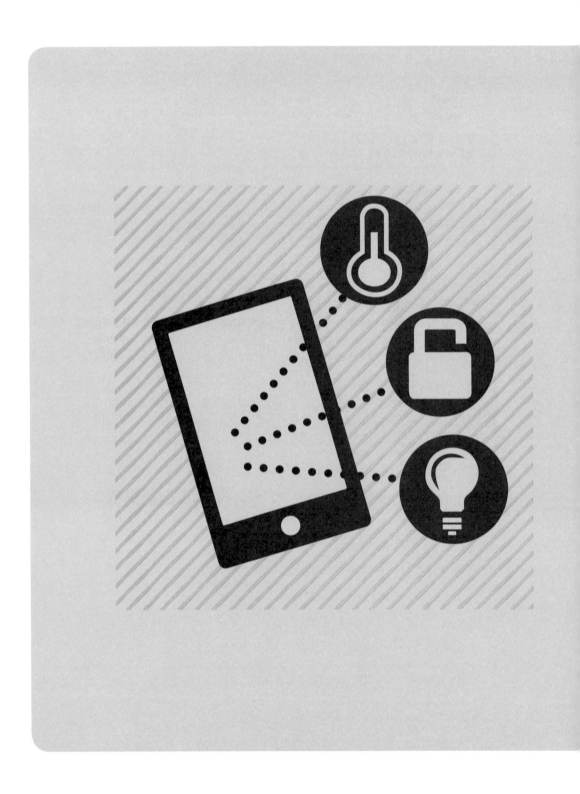

SMART TECH AND TOYS

HOW TO PROTECT YOUR SMART HOME FROM ATTACKERS

WHAT YOU NEED TO KNOW

KAYE'S PERSPECTIVE

We love Alexa in our house; she's a hoot. She was bought as a last-minute Christmas present for our youngest daughter, and pretty soon the whole family was fighting for her attention.

"Alexa, play a song."

"Alexa, switch the light off."

"Alexa, make a rude noise."

"Alexa, give us some quiz questions."

She was so much fun that I was beginning to get dewy-eyed about how great it was to live in the 21st century.

Not long after Alexa arrived, we went out to dinner with friends. I was just about to roll out a hilarious anecdote about the time Alexa broke wind on request when one of our group declared he wouldn't give her houseroom—and not because of her virtual flatulence. It is a listening device, he thundered. It is spying on you and recording everything you say. I actually felt a little bit wounded on Alexa's behalf. Was he crazy? Totally paranoid? Alexa wouldn't do that, would she? When we got home, I didn't speak to Alexa for a while. Was she really a traitor in our midst?

But it's not just Alexa. I can activate and control the TV with my voice; my desktop computer has a built-in camera and microphone; not to mention my iPhone, into which I constantly babble away because I am getting too lazy and myopic to type messages out anymore.

I went and sat in the dark for a while, and it suddenly occurred to me that every time I switch on my computer, no matter what I am looking at, an ad pops up offering "10 Ways to Get Rid of Your Flabby Belly." Maybe it's worse than just listening to me; maybe Alexa can read my mind!

THE "INTERNET OF THINGS"

is the **TERM** that refers to the **PHYSICAL DEVICES** around us that make up our **CONNECTED WORLD**—from Alexas to **REMOTELY ACTIVATED** heating and lights.

WILL'S EXPERT ANALYSIS

Smart tech and the Internet of Things (IoT) is becoming more and more integrated into our lives: our TVs, heating, appliances, and now our kids' toys, too. My concern is our complacency about this—parents rarely consider that these devices potentially open a "virtual doorway" into their home.

There are two areas to worry about, the first of which is security. Many of these new devices connect, directly or indirectly, to the Internet, and often these connections aren't as secure as you might expect. Toys with cameras and microphones, or that send and receive messages, could put your child at risk because hackers can gain control of the device and start communicating with or watching your child, as illustrated in the case study below.

The second concern is about who the device might be sharing information with. A lot of smart tech sends the manufacturer data on how often and in what way the device is being used, which can include recordings and personal information.

How big is the problem?

Smart toys are an emerging market, but we've already seen a lot of high-profile problems. For example, Hasbro's Furby Connect could be exploited by anybody within 33–100 ft (10–30 m) via its Bluetooth

There will be
more than

BILLION
Internet-connected
DEVICES in homes
around the **WORLD**
by **2025.**

WILL'S CASE STUDY

PREDATOR HACKS SMART TOY TO SPEAK TO YOUNG GIRL

One of my colleagues received a call from a distraught father. His 7-year-old daughter kept telling his wife that her doll was talking to her and saying strange things. At first, they thought the child just had a good imagination, because the doll was supposed to say things: it was designed to answer the child's questions by searching online via an Internet connection. So they laughed about it and didn't think anything of it until a few weeks later, when, after their daughter had gone to bed, they heard her talking to somebody—the doll, of course. Then they heard a second voice. A man's voice. The doll had been hacked.

connection, which was a problem if you lived in an apartment building or if you took the toy to public places. Germany has banned several children's smartwatches and the doll Cayla over security concerns, while the Norwegian consumer council found that many Internet-connected toys failed to meet basic consumer standards. In 2017, the FBI sent out an official warning about smart toys, noting that many can be accessed without passwords, PIN codes, or other security checks that prevent strangers from connecting to the device.

Connected appliances are also a potential concern. As smart home technology becomes more common, we should be cautious about how much of our homes and lives we allow it to control. Also make sure that devices viewed remotely via apps are secure.

KAYE:
Okay, Will, now I feel really paranoid—how likely really is it that my smart tech could be hacked? What do we need to be wary about?

WILL:
Anything man-made can be hacked. Change default passwords and tailor your privacy settings.

How could it affect your family?

Children trust and often have conversations with their toys. Toys allow them to practice social interactions. Imagine if a toy was not only speaking back but also enabling a complete stranger to see and talk to your child. It's the stuff of nightmares.

It's not just your child who is at risk: imagine if the rest of your house, from your thermostat to your TV, was recording and possibly videoing what your family said, when you went out, and what you did at home. What if someone accessed all of that data because a device was compromised? You could all be exposed to groomers, extortionists, scammers, or any other kind of online predator.

KAYE:
Will, when I'm buying smart tech, what security features should I look for?

WILL:
Buy from big-name companies and choose devices that have clear privacy details, have regular software updates, and provide encryption.

How do you prevent it from happening?

You need to think about your smart tech and toys in the same way as you would a person you don't know—they can both listen, talk, and see. That's not to say that you shouldn't have smart tech, but if you do, make sure you set it up properly and are in control of it.

Before purchasing, check online reviews of the device, and include the terms "security" or "risks" in the search bar. Many people try to hack these devices for fun and post their findings online for others to see. Also, check the manufacturers' privacy policy. What information does the smart tech share with the manufacturer, and how securely is that information stored?

When you've made a purchase, stick to the rules of smart tech security (see right). If the device is a toy for a child, talk to your child about their new "friend": ask your child questions about what it does, what they talk about, and any strange things the toy does so you can monitor whether the toy is behaving as it should.

What should you do if it's already happened?

If a toy is doing anything unusual, or your child has reported odd behavior, don't take any risks—remove it from your child, disconnect it from the Internet, and switch it off. Check the manufacturer's support section on its website for whether the behavior is a known fault. If not, report the fault on the site, but be aware that it could be something more sinister. Don't use the toy again until you've installed the necessary software updates to fix the vulnerability. How to do this should be explained in the instruction manual or on the manufacturer's website. The same advice applies for smart tech: if you don't trust that it's secure, don't connect it to the Internet or give it to your child until the problem is fixed.

If you think a device has been hacked, consider what it has access to (for example, a smart speaker may be able to read your emails). Change the password for all these accounts—don't assume that if these things haven't been hacked into yet that they won't be in the future. Like identity theft, sometimes the data gleaned from hacked devices isn't used for some time.

When should you seek outside help?

In the case of smart toys, report faults to the manufacturer, but if a device is being exploited by a stranger, this may be a job for the police. Take note of any interactions and any other relevant information. If the toy was connected to the Wi-Fi network, your router may have logged details of incoming connections; if the device connects via Bluetooth, use your phone's Bluetooth menu (in "Settings") to search for other nearby Bluetooth devices and take a screenshot: one of those devices may be being used by the person connecting to the toy. Once you've got as much evidence as possible, take this and the toy to the police.

THE RULES OF SMART TECH SECURITY

Stick to these rules to help keep your family's smart tech and toys secure.

- Always change the default password or PIN code to something new.

- Make sure security settings are configured to limit your child's access—especially for purchases.

- Deactivate any location sharing settings unless absolutely required. If they are on, make sure you know who can see your child's location.

- If the device connects by Bluetooth, search for it with a different device. If it appears, try to change the name to something inconspicuous (e.g., "mouse" or "keyboard").

- Regularly check that the latest software is installed—this will ensure that the device has all of the latest security fixes. You may be able to set it to automatically update.

- Consider where you would or wouldn't let a stranger go with your child (i.e., next to the bath or into a room where your child is changing). You could ban smart toys from these places.

- Cover any cameras with a peelable sticker while they are not in use.

PARENTS' QUESTIONS ANSWERED

I'm really uncomfortable with the idea of phones, tablets, and TVs listening to us all the time. Is it safe to have Google Assistant, Siri, or Alexa?

Officially, yes: all the manufacturers talk about how they take your privacy seriously. However, these companies will use the data collected by your device to improve the performance of their products and better target advertising at you through their platforms and services. Be prepared that, in many cases, they may even sell your data on to third parties for profit, although hopefully they are doing this responsibly.

Be cautious about any technology that doesn't need you to push a button or click OK to connect to the Internet. Anything that listens or watches could be used by others to eavesdrop. Also be wary about allowing Siri to work on a locked screen because this has been exploited to bypass security logins.

KAYE:
So is Alexa listening in on our conversations when she seems to be "asleep"?

WILL:
Most virtual assistants use on-device keyword spotting and will be "asleep" until you use the "wake word." If you're worried, review your recordings in "recording history" and delete them. You can also change the "wake word" to something random.

What exactly are these devices recording?

In most cases, they're looking for particular trigger words or commands, but if they're voice activated, then they could be collecting and storing all kinds of data. In most cases, the processing happens on the manufacturers' computers on their site. For example, in 2015, it emerged that some Samsung smart TVs that had voice recognition were sending audio recordings of their owners to South Korea for analyzing. As soon as the data leaves your device and travels over the Internet, you lose any control over what happens to it. The data that these devices and apps record is often called "metadata," and it's usually tied to an anonymous, meaningless ID made up of a string of letters, numbers, and characters. Because the ID isn't your name, many courts have ruled that metadata doesn't count as personal information. That means firms can share it freely, but you probably gave them permission to do that anyway when you accepted the license agreement that almost nobody ever reads.

This information builds up a really big picture of your life: what you say, what you eat, what you watch on TV, when you go to bed, and so on. Smartwatches now even store data on your heart rate. Would you willingly share all of that information with an advertising company?

Can they collect private data like bank details?

No, but if you've given your card details to the likes of Apple or Amazon, devices such as Alexa can order and pay for items. You card details will usually be encrypted when they're stored, but check how your account is set up: go to "Settings" on the Alexa app then to "Account" and "Voice Purchases" to manage your payment setup, and use strong passwords. You should also check that your devices require a PIN, fingerprint or facial scan, or some form of two-factor authentication (see p.205) to confirm any orders.

That's becoming increasingly important as smart devices place orders by voice. If you don't lock down the payment authorization, your child (or anybody in your home) could order items without your permission. There was a case of a girl in the US asking her parents' Alexa if she could have a dollhouse for Christmas and then receiving the toy from Amazon in the mail. When reporting on the story, a TV presenter repeated the girl's request live on air. The station was innundated with complaints from viewers who had received a dollhouse because their Alexa had heard the presenter on the TV and automatically ordered one.

60% of SMART TECH manufacturers ANALYZE CUSTOMER DATA collected from CONNECTED DEVICES.

Can devices like baby monitors or "nanny cams" also be hacked into?

Yes, they can. Remember, anything with Internet or Wi-Fi connection that records video and audio and isn't made by a big name brand could be hackable. However, some are much easier to access than others.

In 2014, there was a case in which two parents were woken by a stranger screaming through the monitor they used to listen to their 10-month-old baby. The hacker had hijacked the monitor, taking control of its camera and speaker. He screamed at the baby to wake up and then screamed a string of obscenities at the mother.

Old equipment that uses analog rather than digital transmissions is very easy to hack and listen in to using nothing more than a cheap radio scanner. In 2017, more than 60 security cameras made by Canon Inc. were hacked in various locations and rendered unusable. Many of the hacked cameras had messages left on their screens saying, "I'm hacked. bye2."

If you buy any CCTV or nanny cam that you want to view remotely from an app that is connected to your home Wi-Fi, ideally buy equipment that operates on a digital transmission. Many of them use a technology called frequency hopping spread spectrum (FHSS) to change channels randomly, making them even harder for strangers to hack into. If it connects to Wi-Fi, check if the product has any known security risks by checking online reviews. You should also make sure you have a secure Wi-Fi and router password, and change these from the default ones initially set up. Some attacks are on the Wi-Fi router, not directly on the individual devices connected to it.

TAKEAWAYS

1 CHOOSE ROBUST SECURITY
Smart tech devices and toys with minimal security could allow strangers in. Check online reviews, particularly for comments on potential security issues.

2 IMMEDIATELY DISCONNECT SMART TECH OR TOYS THAT ACT ODDLY Check online to see if there is a known problem and whether the manufacturer has released an update to fix it.

3 REPORT SUSPICIOUS BEHAVIOR
If you think someone is using the device to communicate with your child, contact the police.

4 THINK ABOUT HOUSEHOLD CONNECTIONS If you think someone has hacked your smart device or toy, change the passwords of any account it is connected to (e.g., Netflix if it is your smart TV).

5 BE AWARE OF DATA COLLECTION
Your device may be collecting data and sending it back to the manufacturer for analysis (see pp.186–187). This data is generally secure when the device collecting it has been made by a major manufacturer.

6 MONITOR DEVICE VISIBILITY
Check whether your Bluetooth devices are visible by searching for them on another Bluetooth device. If they are, turn on the "invisible" setting in the Bluetooth menu.

7 CHANGE DEFAULT PASSWORDS
Change passwords on cameras, toys, CCTV, Wi-Fi, and routers to new and unique ones.

8 THINK ABOUT LOCATION AND VISIBILITY Put smart tech in family rooms or areas that aren't private, and if you wish, put a sticker over built-in webcam if it's not in use.

WANT MORE INFO? If this chapter hasn't answered all your questions, try:

YOUR CHILD'S DIGITAL FOOTPRINT

THE TRAIL OF PERSONAL INFORMATION YOUR CHILD LEAVES ON THE INTERNET

WHAT YOU NEED TO KNOW

KAYE'S EXPERIENCE

This book was conceived as an aide for parents who want to stay one step ahead of their kids in the online world. As we said at the start, it's nearly impossible to protect your child from danger if you don't understand the dangers yourself.

That said, it's confession time. I am just as much in need of guidance on my digital footprint. Perhaps it's because you are so often alone when you enter the realm of virtual reality that you fool yourself into believing it is private—but make no mistake, it's a tiger's trap. If I'm asked for my zip code or phone number in a shop for its "records," my default response is a polite refusal. Yet somehow I find myself telling wacko websites everything short of my inside leg measurement. As you click away and press "send," it's difficult to imagine what great harm can come of it—as Nadia is fond of saying, your details are but a spit in the ocean. But given what we now know from recent news stories about data gathering and misuse, we are almost obliged to be a bit more savvy.

The single most useful "truth" ever given to me about online activity is, if it's free, then you are the product. I repeat that to my kids time and again in the hope that it implants that note of caution in their heads before they give away their personal information.

As far as not posting anything that might come back to haunt them in later years is concerned, it's not an easy conversation to have with kids. Mine tend to live in the here and now, and trying to get them to appreciate long-term consequences can be the devil's own job. Fortunately, and unfortunately, I have a cautionary tale of my own about an ill-advised Twitter post I sent without a second's thought on a politician, and, gosh, did I feel the repercussions for a long time. It's not just kids who can put their digital foot in it.

Rightly or wrongly, I now stick to the mantra of "positive or bland" for anything that could find its way into the public domain.

WILL'S EXPERT ANALYSIS

Whether we like it or not, so much of our lives are conducted online. Everything that your child uploads on to social media, as well as everything their friends upload about them (including tagging them in a photo or at a certain location), and all the data that companies collect about them is a source of information. This "digital footprint" stays online and could potentially be seen, and judged, by family, future employers, or partners, so this is something children need to be aware of.

Even if neither you nor your child have a social media account, websites that you visit are constantly collecting data about your online activities whenever you search for information, buy products, or interact with someone online. This data can then be used to analyze what products you're likely to buy so that marketing can be specifically targeted at you or your child.

All of this means we need to worry about two things: the information we are passively giving to online data collectors, and how that information about us is being actively shared.

How big is the problem?

Sometimes we don't realize how much we're sharing. Every click, message, post, photo, and "like" is stored somewhere and often made available in ways we didn't expect. It's information like this

KAYE:
But, Will, does it really matter if companies gather data on us? Can't that be quite useful, for example, helping us to streamline our shopping?

WILL:
It's true; it can be useful. But think about the constant nudge from these companies to buy products you've viewed. This can be overwhelming enough for adults, so imagine how the effect is magnified for children, who have less emotional control.

WILL'S CASE STUDY

OFFENSIVE MEMES LEAD TO BOY BEING OSTRACIZED AT SCHOOL

A parent I know discovered his son and his son's friends had been creating and sending images—or "memes"—to each other at school. Somewhat inevitably, the boys had become competitive to see who could create the most offensive image. His son had created and captioned a really horrible and distasteful picture of animal cruelty, which had then been circulated outside of this group to other children. The image was then reported to the teachers. Not only was he punished, but also many of the other children at the school stopped talking to him.

that we often think is private but isn't. Logs of our online activity might be sold on to data analysis companies—businesses that examine our online habits. This analysis is then sold on to online retailers, advertisers, and insurers that target their advertising to increase their sales or improve their businesses. In 2018, it was revealed that some data analysis companies even have political agendas, using social media quizzes to harvest personal data and target wavering voters. This has naturally raised the debate about the culpability of sites that use our data and the need for regulation.

How could it affect your family?

The greatest risk to your child is if they post something offensive, illegal, or even just controversial, and this is linked directly to their real name. This can cause significant reputational damage among peers, friends, and family for days, weeks, months, and sometimes years: potential employers or partners routinely Google names to find out about prospective employees or dates. Some countries even deny access to people they deem as having been offensive online.

If your child's online activity is extensive, you might find that they receive a lot of spam emails (sometimes explicit). This can make them vulnerable to "phishing" attacks (see p.162), through which their data can be stolen or their device infected. Or your child may be inundated with advertisements for products they've viewed, encouraging them to spend money. Data collection companies have even been known to sell on data to insurance or credit rating companies, who analyze whether someone is more of a "risk" from their online activities.

How can you prevent it from happening?

Educate your child so they understand that everything posted online is potentially available forever. This means they shouldn't post anything they wouldn't write in a letter or say to family or friends and ideally never post online when they're angry or upset. Also, they should avoid posting personal details, such as their phone number, home address, or school, or other peoples' details. There are plenty of ways to reduce your child's digital footprint to

---

WHERE IS MY DATA GOING?

Whenever you are online, there is a chance sites will be collecting data about you. This is how the process works:

1. Your data is collected. Many sites charge third parties (data collectors) a fee to collect information on people that visit the site. The data collectors follow site visitors around the web by loading files called "cookies" or "trackers" onto their computers. This allows them to work out which Internet provider you're using, your type of computer or phone, and other identifying information.

2. Your data is aggregated. The information collected is then sold on to data analysis companies. They combine data from different sources to build a detailed picture of you, finding out about your interests, your shopping habits, and sometimes even identifying political opinions.

3. Your data is sold. Analysts sell on their findings to anyone willing to buy them—primarily online advertising companies, but also insurers, credit raters, and political organizations.

prevent sites from tracking them around the Internet. For example, encourage them to avoid doing online surveys and quizzes, regularly delete their Internet cookies (files placed on their computer by websites they visit), or even use software that blocks tracking (see pp.196–197 for more tips). Encourage your child not to use the same username for multiple sites. This makes it harder for others to connect the data from their different online accounts.

What should you do if it's already happened?

If you're aware that your child has put something offensive online, delete it as quickly as possible. On most social media sites, a post is initially visible to friends only (assuming your child has privacy settings). At this stage, the post can be deleted from their page (go to the site admins in the help center if you can't delete it yourself).

If one of their friends takes a screenshot of your child's post and reposts it in a more public place, then it's much more difficult to retrieve. However, most social media platforms can remove the post if you report it, and, if your child is tagged in the post, they can "untag" their name and may even be able to delete it.

If your child starts getting lots of advertisements and spam related to things they have looked at online, they might be sharing too much. Visit the sites your child is registered with and see what personal information they have given the site—this can be visible in the "Your details" or "Your account" section of the site settings. Is your child providing the bare minimum or their whole life story? If you suspect a particular site is selling their data, make minor but noticeable changes—a different email, perhaps.

When should you seek outside help?

Seek help if your child has posted something offensive and there's an online backlash of comments and abuse. Delete the post, and even consider deleting the account. If you can't remove the post, ask the site admins for help—they will be more helpful if they know that the account belongs to a child. Don't worry if your child is below the minimum age for the site; the admins will be used to this and will want to remove your child from their site quickly.

YOUR ONLINE INFORMATION

In the US, there is no legal option available to protect the privacy or request the removal of your online information. (This is different in Europe, where the General Data Protection Regulations act enables citizens to request the removal of personal information stored online from websites operating in the European Union.)

Instead, you have to request the removal of your online information from each company or website separately, and it may or may not respond to your request; they don't all have procedures that let you easily remove your data. In many instances, the only way to remove your data is to delete your account with that site.

Facebook, for example, lets you specify the privacy level of different types of data—visible only to your friends or to the public. To completely remove your data, you have to delete your entire Facebook account. Google, on the other hand, lets you remove certain personal information found in the Google search index. It will not usually remove your date of birth, street addresses, or phone numbers.

PARENTS' QUESTIONS ANSWERED

Are websites really tracking my child around the Internet? How can I stop websites from collecting my child's personal data and online habits?

WHAT DOES SOCIAL MEDIA KNOW?

This is some of the information social media sites may know about your child:

- Full name
- Email address and phone number
- Address/previous addresses
- School/previous schools
- Siblings' and friends' names
- Every post or photo they've ever uploaded (even if deleted)
- Everyone they've tagged in a post or photo
- Every comment they've made and conversation they've had in a chat window on the site or messenger app
- Favorite foods, music, books, movies, sports, celebrities
- Political or religious views

Yes. Lots of them are tracking your child, if not all. Your child's digital footprint is made up of all the personal data that they have entered on various websites. The more pieces of information your child provides, the better the picture the sites have of their life, interests, and habits. There's no sure way to stop all data gathering, but these top tips can help you minimize the data that companies can collect on your child.

- **Tell your child to limit what they share.** When your child registers on a site, encourage them not to give their full name, date of birth, or optional information and to use different usernames for different accounts. If the site needs an email to register, set up a temporary email account that will delete itself after a short period of time. There are many online services that allow you to do this.
- **Tell your child to read the small print.** Many sites ask you to tick boxes to confirm that you don't want them to give away your data, while others ask you to untick them. Make sure your child is careful not to allow the site to give away their personal information.
- **Make sure your child doesn't connect social media accounts to other sites.** An example of this is logging in to an online game through their Facebook account. Your child may not know what information those sites are taking or are sharing from their social media account.

- **Check what your child is sharing on social media.** Regularly log out of their social media accounts to check what a stranger can see on their profile, or download their personal data from social media sites and check this. If something is visible that you think shouldn't be, such as photos, log back on and adjust their privacy settings.
- **Install a VPN (virtual private network; see p.203).** This blocks sites from seeing your child's IP address (the unique number that identifies your device). This number can be sold on to other websites and marketing companies interested in your child's online habits. VPNs are available for laptops, smartphones, and tablets.
- **Check your child's cookies.** Cookies are files stored on the web browser of their computer so that sites can identify them and remember their settings from previous visits. Go to your child's browser settings, and then select "Privacy." Choose which cookies you want to allow—some cookies store preferences and do actually improve site visits—and block any unwanted third-party cookies (which come from sites you haven't actually visited). You can also do this for the browser on their smartphone or tablet.
- **Don't complete online surveys or do online quizzes.** Some of the biggest privacy breaches come from people filling out innocuous-looking surveys or doing fun-sounding quizzes. These often collect personal information and leave trackers on your computer.
- **Google your child.** Put your child's name in quotation marks (for example, "John Smith") to see what comes up when people search for their name. If you find anything you don't want shared, go to that site and delete the information. If it can't be deleted, change it to fake information or ask the site admins to remove it.

If you want to see which organizations are tracking your child, there are clever apps, such as Ghostery, that you can install on their web browser.

MANY SITES YOU VISIT are **PAID** by other **SITES** you **HAVEN'T** visited to place **COOKIES** on your web browser. These are called **THIRD-PARTY** cookies.

My son isn't scared to say what he thinks online, but I'm worried his social media posts will look bad to employers in a few years' time.

It's wise to worry. Checking job applicants' Internet "footprint"—what comes up in searches against their name—and social media history is very common in recruitment. A company's reputation is vital, so they don't want something an employee said or did to bring the company into disrepute or for an employee to appear online to be someone they wouldn't want working for them.

That means it's essential for your son to understand that a silly, immature post on social media could come back and seriously affect his life by damaging his reputation or his chance of getting his dream job.

And it's not just his posts. It's his replies to his friends' posts, his comments on videos, and the posts he "liked" or "upvoted." All that information is stored, even the private stuff. Some social networks even record the messages you type but change your mind about sending. He can't be sure that what's private today is really private, or will stay private forever. He needs to think every time, "What's the worst possible way somebody could interpret this?" If in doubt, leave it out.

In 2018, it was estimated that

90%

of **EMPLOYERS** hiring staff **CHECKED** the **DIGITAL FOOTPRINT** of **JOB APPLICANTS.**

TAKEAWAYS

1 TELL YOUR CHILD TO THINK BEFORE THEY POST Are they saying anything they might regret later? Tell them to remember that posts could stay online even after they've deleted them.

2 ENCOURAGE YOUR CHILD NOT TO OVERSHARE They should give websites only the information they need, not provide any optional data, and never give away personal details—their own or someone else's.

3 CHECK YOUR CHILD'S ONLINE PRIVACY SETTINGS Delete third-party "cookies" from sites they haven't visited, and consider using a private network (VPN) to hide their browsing activity from websites.

4 CLEAR YOUR CHILD'S COOKIES REGULARLY Check the cookies loaded on their web browser and clear these to stop specific sites from tracking them.

5 QUICKLY DELETE POTENTIALLY OFFENSIVE POSTS If you can't access the post, ask the site administrators to remove it.

6 TELL YOUR CHILD NOT TO "CONNECT" SOCIAL MEDIA ACCOUNTS Logging on to one site via another account helps sites to build a picture of your child.

7 GOOGLE YOUR CHILD Check what others can see. Are they giving too much away, or are they in posts they're not even aware of?

8 AVOID FREEBIES Games, quizzes, and trials all come at a price—often your child's personal identity.

9 VARY USERNAMES Don't use the same username across multiple sites. This allows people to connect personal information gathered on you from different places.

WANT MORE INFO? If this chapter hasn't answered all your questions, try:

DEVICE SAFETY AND SECURITY

SETTING UP DEVICES AND ONLINE ACCOUNTS FOR MAXIMUM SAFETY

SETTING UP A SECURE DEVICE

Your child's device may be used for banking, shopping, socializing, and more. How you set up a device, from the moment you take it out of the box, can make all the difference to the level of risk you or your child could be exposed to. Technology moves rapidly, and new innovations occur almost daily, but there are some fundamental procedures you can follow to protect your child's device, keeping intruders out and safeguarding private information. Check that your child's existing devices follow these recommendations, too.

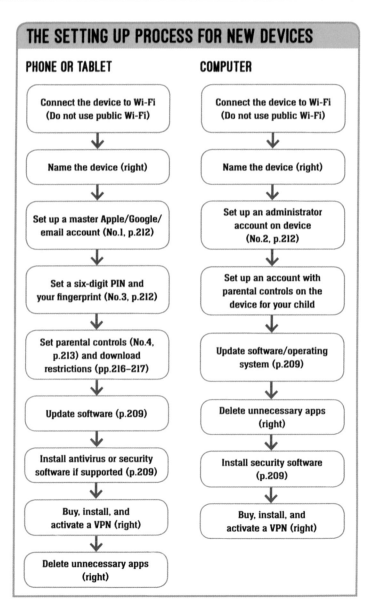

THE SETTING UP PROCESS FOR NEW DEVICES

PHONE OR TABLET

- Connect the device to Wi-Fi (Do not use public Wi-Fi)
- Name the device (right)
- Set up a master Apple/Google/email account (No.1, p.212)
- Set a six-digit PIN and your fingerprint (No.3, p.212)
- Set parental controls (No.4, p.213) and download restrictions (pp.216–217)
- Update software (p.209)
- Install antivirus or security software if supported (p.209)
- Buy, install, and activate a VPN (right)
- Delete unnecessary apps (right)

COMPUTER

- Connect the device to Wi-Fi (Do not use public Wi-Fi)
- Name the device (right)
- Set up an administrator account on device (No.2, p.212)
- Set up an account with parental controls on the device for your child
- Update software/operating system (p.209)
- Delete unnecessary apps (right)
- Install security software (p.209)
- Buy, install, and activate a VPN (right)

NAME YOUR DEVICE

Avoid giving away personal details in a device's name. Your child's device is potentially visible to others when they connect to the Internet or have Bluetooth active. Choose a name that's ambiguous, indeterminable, and asexual to avoid revealing your child's name and identity.

GOOD EXAMPLES

AAA — A repeated letter

Random letters and numbers — **Z123d**

BAD EXAMPLE

Reveals name and purpose of device → **Jane Smith's work laptop**

DELETE UNNECESSARY APPS

Preinstalled apps and programs can increase the vulnerability of your child's devices. Often new or used Android devices or Windows laptops come preloaded with "bloatware"—many can be unnecessary apps that slow down your child's device or compromise their privacy. Remove anything that they don't want to use. Some can be useful, but if in doubt, search for reviews by other users.

ACTIVATE A VPN

Using a VPN (virtual private network) secures connections. A VPN conceals your IP address (your computer's ID number when online). This can help protect your child's identity and location and makes it harder for anyone tracking, intercepting, or stealing your child's data. Your child can therefore use public Wi-Fi more safely. VPNs can be used on phones and tablets, too. VPNs are generally subscription services, so you will need to choose and buy one. Make sure that you install software updates for your child's VPN regularly (or even set it to "auto update") to keep their device secure.

HOW A VPN PROTECTS DATA

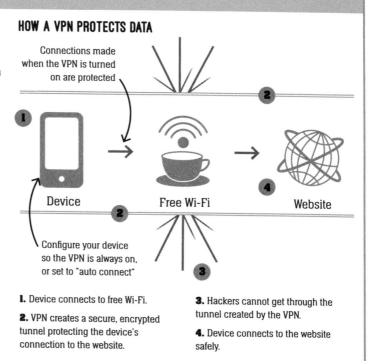

Connections made when the VPN is turned on are protected

1 Device

2 Free Wi-Fi

Website

4

Configure your device so the VPN is always on, or set to "auto connect"

3

1. Device connects to free Wi-Fi.

2. VPN creates a secure, encrypted tunnel protecting the device's connection to the website.

3. Hackers cannot get through the tunnel created by the VPN.

4. Device connects to the website safely.

USING PASSWORDS AND "PASSPHRASES"

Passwords are our first defense when protecting our devices and personal data, so they need to be strong and secure. A strong password on your child's device(s) is essential. If their password is guessed or hacked, then the hacker will have access to any auto-saved passwords or information on the device.

Passwords should be complex, or even an entire phrase, such as a song lyric or a line from a film or poem. Simple, single-word passwords can be cracked by hackers in minutes, if not seconds.

It is also essential that you change the default password provided for a device. This includes any smart tech, CCTV, and your home Wi-Fi router.

1 CREATE COMPLEX PASSWORDS

The safest, hardest-to-crack passwords have several elements. Can your child's passwords be easily guessed? A pet's name, a favorite sports team, or a celebrity? Use something more unexpected, and add symbols and numbers. Try using an online password generator if you're feeling stumped.

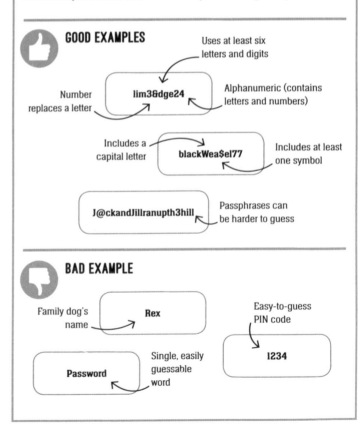

GOOD EXAMPLES

lim36dge24
- Uses at least six letters and digits
- Number replaces a letter
- Alphanumeric (contains letters and numbers)

blackWea$el77
- Includes a capital letter
- Includes at least one symbol

J@ckandJillranupth3hill
- Passphrases can be harder to guess

BAD EXAMPLE

Rex
- Family dog's name

Password
- Single, easily guessable word

1234
- Easy-to-guess PIN code

2 MAKE EACH PASSWORD DIFFERENT

Using a different password for each account reduces risk.
The more unique passwords your child has, the fewer you'll have to reset if one is hacked. Many sites have a "forgot password" option if needed, or use an app that stores and encrypts passwords if your child can't remember them.

3 SET UP SECURITY QUESTIONS

Personalize security answers so these are difficult to guess.
Some sites require you to enter recovery questions to set up an account, but the answers to these questions can often be guessed or found out. To avoid this, choose a random answer and note it down in a safe place.

GOOD EXAMPLES

Q: What is your mother's maiden name?
A: Star Wars
↳ Mother's favorite film

Q: What was your first pet's name?
A: Fiat Punto
↳ First car

4 ENABLE TWO-FACTOR AUTHENTICATION

Using a second password increases online security.
Two-factor authentication (2FA) is a system that requires anyone logging into an account to enter two passwords—the main password and a second, randomly generated code sent via text.

If 2FA is activated on your child's online accounts, no one can sign in as your child unless they have the password and your child's phone. Your child will also know if someone is trying to log in to their account because they will get a text message with a new passcode.

For younger children, enter your phone number instead so that your child can't change the password or parental controls or log in from a different device.

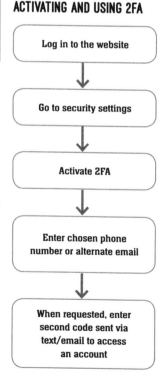

ACTIVATING AND USING 2FA

Log in to the website
↓
Go to security settings
↓
Activate 2FA
↓
Enter chosen phone number or alternate email
↓
When requested, enter second code sent via text/email to access an account

5 SECURE SAVED PASSWORDS

Saving passwords is fine if your overall security is good.
Using the "save password" option for online accounts is generally safe if the device's password is strong and you use 2FA (see No.4) for online shopping. You could use a password app instead (see No.2).

6 CHANGE PASSWORDS FREQUENTLY

Regularly updating passwords protects your data.
Ideally, change passwords every few months. This will protect your child if their account has been hacked without their knowledge.

BEST PRACTICES

Your child's device might be protected by the most impenetrable software and their device and web accounts individually password protected, but that doesn't prevent accidents, system failures, unpredictable breaches, or just poor housekeeping and maintenance from causing problems. Here are some basic user guidelines.

BACKING UP YOUR DEVICE

Setting up a reliable backup system is a top priority.
Whether your child drops their device, spills a drink on it, loses it, changes the password and forgets what they changed it to, it is stolen or hacked, or their device simply goes wrong, if you have backed up the device, the only data they will lose is whatever they've done between the last backup and the time their device became unavailable. There are two options for backing up their software and data: the cloud or an external hard drive.

USING THE CLOUD
Backing up their data via the Internet is a reliable option.
The cloud is a network of servers that stores data on the Internet. Stored data is encrypted, so it is generally very secure. Your child can access their data on any device with an Internet connection.

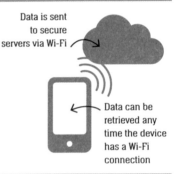

Data is sent to secure servers via Wi-Fi

Data can be retrieved any time the device has a Wi-Fi connection

USING A HARD DRIVE
An external hard drive is a convenient way to back up data.
Computers can be backed up to external hard drives, while phones and tablets can often be backed up to computers using the correct software (e.g., using iTunes to back up an iPhone). Solid state hard drives (SSDs) are the most robust. If you use an external hard drive to back up the computer, make sure it is encrypted with a password so that if the hard drive is lost or stolen, the data can't be accessed.

Ideally, back up your child's device each night. This may take a while the first time but then should speed up if you back up regularly. Keep the hard drive somewhere safe and in a separate place from the computer.

LOCATION TRACKING

The ability to track your child's device can be useful in certain circumstances.
Most devices have built-in tracking software. This means that if your child's device is lost or stolen, you can track it from any web browser using the the Apple or Google account you logged into on it. Some versions of the software allow you to send the device a message that appears on the locked screen or to wipe it remotely to avoid data theft.

Apps that can transmit your child's location to others, such as Find My Friends, should be treated with caution. Check your settings to see if an app is requesting permission to use your location, decide if this is something you definitely need, and then if in doubt, switch the feature off. Websites and software such as MyPermissions.com also allow you to check whether your apps are accessing any other personal information.

HOW TO TURN OFF LOCATION SETTINGS ON APPS

```
Settings
   ↓
Privacy
   ↓
Location services
   ↓          ↘
Select "Only while using"    Select "Off"
for practical apps, such     for all other apps
as maps
          ↘          ↙
Check "System services" and select "Off" for
elements you don't want to access your location
```

HOW TO TRACK YOUR DEVICE

Locating and possibly disabling your phone protects your data.
Device-finding services allow you to carry out some functions on your phone from any web browser.

1 Track—See where the device is on a map and check its remaining battery.

2 Alert—The device will make a noise so you can find it if you are nearby.

3 Lock—This prevents anyone who has picked up the device from opening it. Some systems allow you to display a message on the device's lock screen.

4 Erase—The contents of the device are wiped. This may be necessary if you suspect the device has been stolen and you want to protect your child's data.

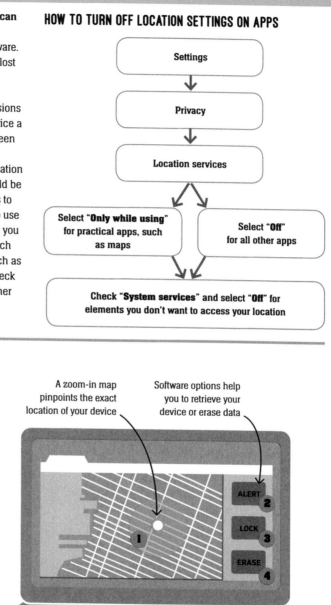

A zoom-in map pinpoints the exact location of your device

Software options help you to retrieve your device or erase data

ALERT **2**
LOCK **3**
ERASE **4**

PUBLIC AND FREE WI-FI CONNECTIONS

Free Wi-Fi connections are convenient but very risky.
Be particularly cautious about a Wi-Fi network that doesn't require a password—this could be a scam network set up by a hacker. Connecting to a hacker's network allows them to intercept data, including bank card details if you are shopping online. You may also be at risk of the hacker breaking directly into your device.

It's best to set your child's phone to "Ask before connecting to unknown networks" in the Wi-Fi menu (in Settings) of your child's device to ensure that the device connects only to safe networks.

PROTECTION FROM HACKERS

A VPN or using mobile data protects your child from hackers.
One effective way to protect your child from hackers is to install a VPN on your device (see p.203).

If they don't have a VPN, they can use their mobile data, since this creates a more secure connection. They can even connect their laptop to their cell phone data by turning on their device's hotspot or tethering function in the settings menu. Before they use their device as a hotspot, check the service provider's terms and conditions to see if there is an extra charge for this. Also, bear in mind that their computer will use up data far more quickly than their phone does, since a laptop will access the full versions of websites rather than the smaller, mobile versions their phone connects to.

TURN YOUR SMARTPHONE INTO A WI-FI HOTSPOT

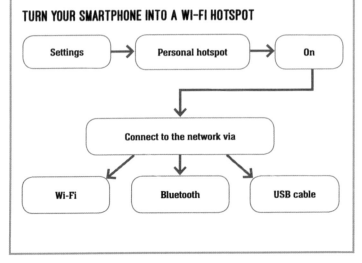

USING BLUETOOTH

Ensure your device isn't visible to other Bluetooth users.
Bluetooth is often used to connect keyboards or speakers to a device, or an earpiece to talk while traveling.

However, Bluetooth can also display your device name to anyone else using Bluetooth within your proximity. This can leave your child's device open to attacks known as "bluejacking" (or "bluehacking"). Although this doesn't compromise their data, it can enable a stranger to send them unsolicited messages. Your child should only turn on Bluetooth when they are actually using it, and that check only their devices are connected.

VISIBLE DEVICES

Devices are visible to other people when Bluetooth is on.
Ensure that your child's device name doesn't give them away. You can change it in Settings.

SOFTWARE UPDATES

Regularly updating software improves its efficiency.

In addition to installing antivirus software on your child's device (see right), install updates for the operating system (OS) of their device (the software that allows your device to function and run other programs).

Computer and device manufacturers constantly check and test their devices and release software updates to reduce crashing and improve security. If your child doesn't have "auto update" enabled on their device, they will receive a message telling them that an update is available. Back up your child's device before they install the update.

In addition to these general updates, make sure that you also regularly update your antivirus software, too.

INSTALL SECURITY SOFTWARE

Purchase antivirus software and enable preinstalled protection.

No device is invulnerable to viruses and malware. To catch these problems before they do any damage, buy and install antivirus software on all your child's devices.

Also be sure to turn on any built-in "firewall"—a preinstalled system on most computers that protects against viruses and malware.

Most cell phones don't have a built-in firewall, but you can download an app for some. Do some online research to find the best one for your device.

SETTING UP PROTECTION

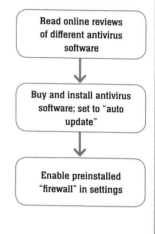

Read online reviews of different antivirus software

↓

Buy and install antivirus software; set to "auto update"

↓

Enable preinstalled "firewall" in settings

WHAT TO DO IF A DEVICE IS JAILBROKEN OR ROOTED

Jailbreaking puts your child's device and data at risk from malicious apps.

Jailbreaking (or "rooting") is when a phone or tablet's operating system is modified to load unapproved apps and programs. This will destroy the built-in security and puts any personal data on the device at risk. If you suspect your child's phone has been jailbroken, or your child has jailbroken their device to get unapproved apps, reset the device back to factory settings and return the data from the latest backup.

RESET APPLE DEVICES

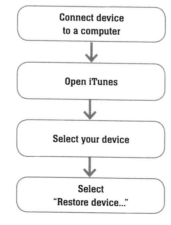

Connect device to a computer

↓

Open iTunes

↓

Select your device

↓

Select "Restore device..."

RESET ANDROID DEVICES

Android phones and tablets have a range of unrooting methods depending on what device you own. Look up how to unroot your specific device online.

MANAGING YOUR CHILD'S ONLINE ACCESS

WHAT TO CONSIDER

How you decide to manage your child's access to devices and the Internet depends on their age, your child's level of maturity, and your own parenting style. You may be happy that your child is sufficiently mature and trustworthy to be allowed unsupervised online access. However, it's also important to be aware of the dangers inherent to children on the Internet. Children will explore without the foresight and experience that adults have; this means they may not be able to identify risks, and as a consequence they may be exposed to unsuitable or upsetting content.

It's sensible, therefore, to set clear parameters and safe boundaries that allow your child to enjoy the benefits of the Internet while also protecting them from its dangers. There are several options for setting ground rules and restrictions and various ways you can manage, supervise, and control your child's digital devices and online activities (see pp.228–229).

REUSED DEVICES

If you are recycling one of your old devices, back up all your old data and either reset it to the factory settings or erase everything.

If you are buying a second-hand model, make sure it is not so old that software updates are no longer available for it. Check that it has been restored to factory settings before you buy it so that you don't inherit something bad from the previous owner. You may want to restore factory settings again yourself to ensure that the device is clean.

CHOOSING YOUR SYSTEM

There are two ways to manage your child's access to the Internet: you can either share your device or give your child exclusive use of their own device. The chart below looks at the pros and cons to both of these approaches on different devices. Decide which system works best for you and your child.

	COMPUTER	SMARTPHONE/TABLET
SHARING	• You can easily set up a guest account for your child on your own computer. A guest account restricts your child from having access to your personal information and websites and allows you to retain overall control. • Most antivirus software and VPNs installed on the computer will work across all the accounts, so your child's data will be protected. • Ensuring that parental controls are working for your child's account means you can be confident that your child is not using your passwords for online accounts or shopping, or viewing your private data.	• You can't set up a guest account for your child on a smartphone or tablet so your child will potentially have full access to everything on your device. This includes email accounts, documents, apps, saved bank cards, photos, movies, and music. • You shouldn't share your device with your child if you use it for work. Even if your child doesn't intend to, they could delete or tamper with your work email account, folders, or files. • For younger children, share your phone or tablet only if you are with them and you can explore sites together in a fully supervised capacity.
EXCLUSIVE USE	• Having their own computer can be useful for older children who may need increased access to a computer for schoolwork. Parental controls can be set on the computer, but it can be harder to govern the amount of time your child is spending online. • You may want to set yourself up as the administrator account on the computer and give your child a separate account. This will allow you to maintain control over program installation and certain parental control settings.	• You may decide to give your child their own phone or tablet to use at the appropriate age and when they've demonstrated responsibility. This means you can keep in touch with your child when they're outside the home and avoid the disruption of sharing your own device. • When setting up their device, follow the guidance on p.202 to ensure you maintain control over it.

GENERAL PARENTAL CONTROLS

These guidelines will help you set up general passwords and controls across all the devices that your child uses as well as help you set up their social media and email accounts and advise on photography, videos, and shopping.

1 SET UP A MASTER ACCOUNT

A master account can help you to manage your child's smartphone or tablet.
I recommend setting up a new iCloud or Google account specifically for your child's device. You might also want to set up a new email account specifically to manage the device. This can be linked to the new iCloud or Google account. Only you should know the password for these accounts. Make sure that your child cannot access the email inbox from the device, since this could allow them to reset the password to the account and make purchases or change parental controls.

2 CREATE COMPUTER ACCOUNTS

As account administrator, you can control access to services. Ensure that only you have the password for the administrator account on any computer that your child is using. They should have their own nonadminstrator account, which you can set restrictions on, such as web filters. You should also know their passwords and have access to all areas of the computer, including emails and social media.

3 DEVICE PASSCODE AND FINGERPRINT

Be in control of the password for your child's device.
Whether you are sharing a device or giving your child their own, you need to set a password to unlock it (see pp.204–205).
For younger children, set a password that only you know so that you can control when they use the device and for how long. As your child gets older, you may choose to share the password so they can access the device on their own.
If the device has a fingerprint scanner, make sure that only your fingerprint is registered; registering your child's fingerprint may allow them to make purchases and download apps without entering the Apple or Google account password (see pp.216–217).

 **SET PARENTAL CONTROLS ON DEVICES**

Like computers, tablets and phones have parental controls. Within Settings on all tablets and phones, there is a section for parental controls, which require a PIN number to alter. This PIN will generally be different from that required to unlock the device. Set up these controls before you give your child access to the tablet or phone. If you share the device, you need to switch the restrictions back off again when you want to use it.

SET CONTROLS ON IPHONE

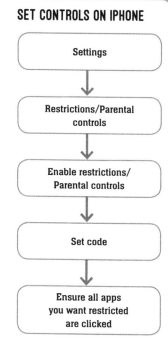

Settings
↓
Restrictions/Parental controls
↓
Enable restrictions/ Parental controls
↓
Set code
↓
Ensure all apps you want restricted are clicked

THIRD-PARTY PARENTAL CONTROL APPS

Apps can help you set up robust parental controls. Some "third-party" apps can impose parental controls on your child's device. These might set time limits for online use, filter content, block sites, and monitor messages and webcams. Before you install one of these apps, read user reviews online, and download only from reputable online stores. Don't install apps that need you to jailbreak your child's phone; doing so will leave their device open to security risks and could void the warranty (see p.209).

SETTING UP YOUR CHILD'S EMAIL ACCOUNT

Your child needs an email account to sign up to websites. Children often have their own email account to communicate with friends and sign up for other online accounts. Decide on a username with your child. This will be the central account from which they can control all their online activity. Make sure only you know their password, set 2FA (see p.205) and load the account onto your device so that you can access their inbox.

WHAT TO THINK ABOUT

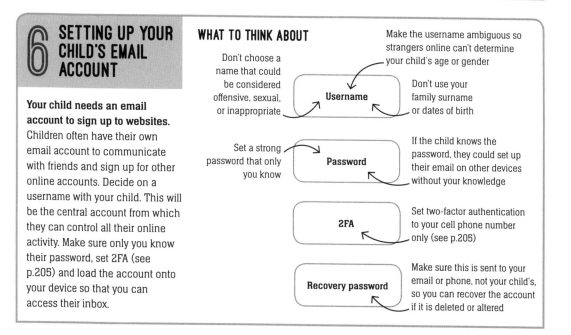

Username

Don't choose a name that could be considered offensive, sexual, or inappropriate

Make the username ambiguous so strangers online can't determine your child's age or gender

Don't use your family surname or dates of birth

Password

Set a strong password that only you know

If the child knows the password, they could set up their email on other devices without your knowledge

2FA

Set two-factor authentication to your cell phone number only (see p.205)

Recovery password

Make sure this is sent to your email or phone, not your child's, so you can recover the account if it is deleted or altered

7 SETTING UP DEVICE LOCATION

Link location-finding software to your own email.
Make sure any preinstalled, "Find My Phone" software is enabled (see p.207) on your child's device and that it is set to your parental administrative email account. This will enable you to manage events if the device is lost or stolen.

8 YOUR CHILD'S MESSAGING SERVICES

Monitoring online chat can alert you to potential problems.
Choosing a messaging service that links to your desktop means you can keep an eye on your child's online chat. Services such as WhatsApp, Skype, and Apple's iMessage all have desktop or web browser versions that enable you to see your child's messages. Be aware that some apps have a "secret messaging" option, which means conversations won't show up on the browser app.

VIEW MESSAGES ON DESKTOP

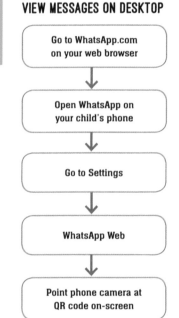

Go to WhatsApp.com on your web browser

↓

Open WhatsApp on your child's phone

↓

Go to Settings

↓

WhatsApp Web

↓

Point phone camera at QR code on-screen

9 PURCHASING ONLINE

Control any online purchases your child makes.
It's important to regulate any online puchases your child makes. Don't authorize your child on your bank cards or allow them access to your PayPal accounts, and avoid setting up "auto fill" payment details. Ensure that your online shopping accounts all have 2FA enabled (see p.205) and that verification passwords or passphrases are required before any purchases can be completed (see pp.216–217).

10 YOUR CHILD'S SOCIAL MEDIA

The correct privacy settings can protect your child.
Most of the major social media accounts have minimum age limits, but these are often ignored and are poorly monitored by the sites. If your child is eager to have a social media account but too young to sign up themselves, you could suggest setting up a family social media page initially. This will allow your child to post or message family and friends on the account but lets you monitor who they connect with. You can control the password and set the recovery email to your own email.

For older children, ensure that your child's social media page has strong privacy settings, with information shared with friends only and that they don't provide or post personal information. View their account while logged out to see what information your child is sharing with people who aren't their friends.

11 YOUTUBE, VIMEO, AND VIDEO STREAMING

Streaming sites may not have age restrictions in place.
Many streaming sites, such as YouTube, don't have parental controls unless you sign in. To ensure that your child cannot access adult content on YouTube, don't sign in to your email on your child's device (see below), and regularly check that your child hasn't created a separate email account to access adult content.

MAKE SURE TO LOG OUT OF YOUR PERSONAL EMAIL

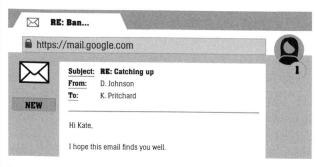

Logging in to certain accounts gives you access to multiple sites (for example, your Google account is the same as your YouTube account). You can see who is logged in from the image in the top right of the screen (1).

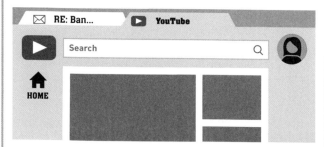

If you log in to your Google account to check your email on your child's device, they will automatically be logged in as you when they open YouTube. This can give them access to adult-rated content depending on your settings.

12 MONITORING ONLINE SEARCHES

Check your child's history to monitor their viewing.
Most devices enable Private Browsing, which hides online search history. You can set restrictions on many devices to block adult content, although these are not infallible. Talk to your child about what they should and shouldn't view online. Say that their browsing history always needs to be visible and that they should never clear it. Explain that you trust them to honor this and that you will have to impose restrictions on their device usage (or confiscate it entirely) if they do clear their Internet history.

13 MONITORING YOUR CHILD'S APPS

Keep your child safe by making sure they are using safe apps.
Monitor the apps your child has on their device (see pp.216–217). Research any that look suspicious or are not easily identifiable. For example, some apps that look like utilities actually enable secret messaging or hide photos. If you find a dubious-looking app, ask your child what it's for. If they're unwilling to explain and open it in front of you, delete it.

MONITORING APP DOWNLOADS

To ensure that your child can't purchase apps without your permission, set up the device's master account (Apple or Google account) with your dedicated email address (see No.1, p.212), and make sure that this account has 2FA enabled (see p.205). This

FREE APPS

The instructions below show you how to restrict or permit free app downloads.
If you do allow your child to download free apps, make sure that they are aware
of dangers such as hidden subscriptions or malware.

FREE APPS ON YOUR APPLE DEVICES

FREE APPS ON ANDROID

This is not childproof, and it doesn't stop your child from viewing an app, but the app will display a message saying that it can't be downloaded without the PIN (see right).

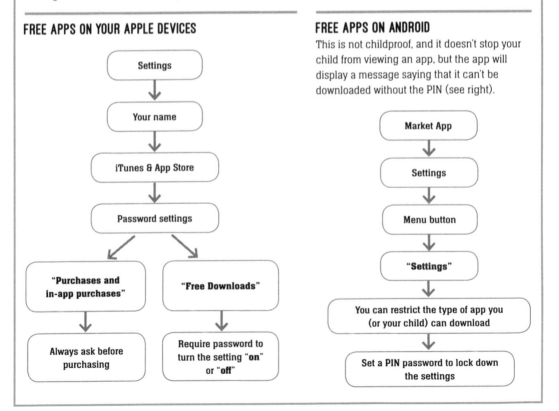

FREE APPS ON YOUR APPLE DEVICES

Settings
↓
Your name
↓
iTunes & App Store
↓
Password settings
↙ ↘
"Purchases and in-app purchases" | "Free Downloads"
↓ | ↓
Always ask before purchasing | Require password to turn the setting "on" or "off"

FREE APPS ON ANDROID

Market App
↓
Settings
↓
Menu button
↓
"Settings"
↓
You can restrict the type of app you (or your child) can download
↓
Set a PIN password to lock down the settings

means you will be emailed whenever an app is downloaded or a purchase attempt is made, so you will know if your child has discovered or circumvented the password.

IN-APP PURCHASES

Follow the steps below to restrict and/or control in-app purchases from online stores, social media marketplaces, and auction sites.

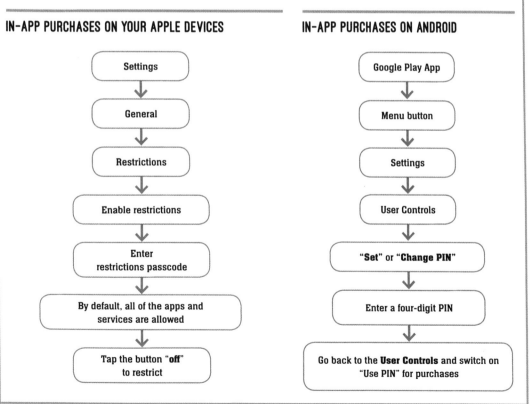

IN-APP PURCHASES ON YOUR APPLE DEVICES

Settings
↓
General
↓
Restrictions
↓
Enable restrictions
↓
Enter restrictions passcode
↓
By default, all of the apps and services are allowed
↓
Tap the button "**off**" to restrict

IN-APP PURCHASES ON ANDROID

Google Play App
↓
Menu button
↓
Settings
↓
User Controls
↓
"**Set**" or "**Change PIN**"
↓
Enter a four-digit PIN
↓
Go back to the **User Controls** and switch on "Use PIN" for purchases

IT'S ALL GONE WRONG

WHEN YOU NEED TO CALL IN OUTSIDE HELP

WHO TO CONTACT AND WHEN

BRINGING IN THIRD PARTIES

This page will help you determine whether you can resolve things yourself or need to get other parties involved. If you need to contact your child's school or the police, then you should gather evidence of what has happened first (see pp.226–227).

KEEP IT IN THE FAMILY

There's no need to call the police if your child has made a simple mistake or hasn't done anything damaging. Many problems can be solved by deleting offending posts, closing a social media account, or deleting a folder of illegally downloaded content and then explaining to your child how (and why) to avoid any reoccurrences.

TELL ANOTHER PARENT

If the problem has also been caused by, or with the help of, another child, both children need to understand the consequences of their actions. Speak to another parent if their child has:

- Ganged up with your child to bully or cyberbully another child
- Exchanged illegal products or illegal content with your child
- Exchanged pornographic or explicit material with your child
- Shared or received your child's or another child's nude images
- Sold something to your child and not delivered what they'd sold
- Shared how-tos on eating disorders, self-harm, suicide, or violence with your child (see also "Get your child a counselor," right)

CONTACT THE SCHOOL

Contact your child's school if the issue started at school or involves more than one other student. The teachers may be able to step in, prevent the problem from spreading, and help resolve it quickly. They may have dealt with similar incidents before and be in a position to talk to you about whether you need to escalate the situation further or find your child a counselor. It also gives the school an opportunity to educate its students about the dangers of the issue.

GET YOUR CHILD A COUNSELOR

I believe it's essential to refer your child to a counselor in the following circumstances:

- They appear oblivious to the seriousness of the situation.
- They refuse to talk about the problem, or their behavior becomes physically or psychologically problematic when they do.
- They start habitually downloading illegal material.
- They start self-harming or being cruel to siblings, pets, or others.

When you refer the matter to a counselor, provide as much information as you can by sharing any of the evidence you have. See p.232 for a list of agencies that can help find a counselor.

CALL THE POLICE

Contacting the police is a last resort—hopefully you can solve most problems before it comes to this. If you know the perpetrator, speaking to their parent or teacher may be sufficient. If this doesn't work, state that you will contact the police if the situation continues. If the perpetrator is an adult, you should immediately report them to the police if they have:

- Solicited sexual conversation, images, or activity from your child
- Requested that your child meet them offline in secret or without your knowledge
- Threatened to physically harm, injure, or kill your child
- Offered your child pharmaceuticals or illegal drugs
- Persistently abused or harassed your child
- Sent or received child pornography (see p.225)
- Extorted money from or blackmailed your child

The above list isn't comprehensive. Bear in mind that it's especially important for you speak to the police if the perpetrator is an adult, because they may be targeting other children, too.

DON'T PANIC!

If you are here, it may be because you want to prepare yourself for issues or because things have gone wrong already. If the latter, take a deep breath, make yourself a cup of tea or coffee, and read on. You can solve the problem! Try to break it down into these four steps:

1. Ask what happened. Find out as much as you can—what took place, how it happened, how your child was involved, who else is involved, and what effect it's having on your child and your family (see p.18). Knowing all of this will help you gather evidence for later on.

2. Take control. What has happened is done; now you need to take control. That might mean taking away your child's device until the problem has been solved.

3. Limit the damage. You've stopped the immediate issue; now work out whether more problems could occur. Do you need to change your child's password or delete an infected file from their device?

4. Resolve the issue. The final step requires time and effort. Ensure that the problem can't reoccur—have compromising images all been deleted? Have you changed your child's passwords? In serious cases, you may need to report the perpetrator to the school or the police (see left).

DEALING WITH ILLEGAL CONTENT

LEVELS OF ILLEGALITY

There are lots of laws that cover the Internet and the content available on it. We've looked in detail at this in relevant chapters, but the list on the right of this page should act as a quick reference. The severity of a particular crime is generally determined by what the perpetrator did with the illegal material or product.

WHAT THEY SEE AND DOWNLOAD

Nobody will be prosecuted for accidentally seeing something they shouldn't, but downloading illegal material or regularly visiting sites that contain illegal material is another matter.

Many websites are age restricted (for example, gambling sites). This makes it illegal for minors to view them, especially if your child is pretending to be older than they are, or even pretending to be someone else entirely.

It is illegal to download copyrighted movies, television shows, games, and apps without paying for them. The risk of prosecution is small, but the fines are massive. Also, your Internet service provider can limit your Internet connection if it finds someone using your Internet connection is illegally downloading a lot of material.

It is a very serious criminal offense in most parts of the world to view or download explicit images of minors (see box, p.225).

It's also worth noting that some countries have strong anti-terror laws that mean just reading certain books or websites will bring your child to the attention of the authorities.

WHAT THEY PAY FOR

The police consider paying to access a site containing illegal material as a clear indication that you viewed it intentionally.

When it comes to illegal products (such as drugs or weapons), it matters where the product is rather than where it came from.

Your child could be prosecuted for buying something that's illegal in the country in which they receive it, even if it's not illegal in the country from which they bought it.

This is the same for online content—it's the legality of the content where they access it rather than where it was uploaded.

WHAT THEY SHARE

Sharing illegal material is more serious than just viewing it, and, in most parts of the world, the penalties can be life changing. It's unlikely that your child will be sent to prison for downloading movies illegally, but if they are running a website that people use to watch or download movies, it's a different story.

When it comes to online harassment, bullying, or hate speech, something that might be legal on its own could become illegal in the context of a wider set of posts. For example, when it comes to online harassment, one mean comment or message is unlikely to be illegal. However, if that one mean comment comes in a series of four or more mean comments, messages, or posts sent to a particular person over a short period of time, the police can interpret that as harassment, which is illegal.

Starting a parody account could also be illegal—this may break laws on defamation (lying to damage someone else's reputation).

PARENTAL LIABILITY

If your child is doing something illegal online and you know about it but don't try to stop them, you could be liable for prosecution.

This can fall under the "tort of negligent control," where a parent can be held liable if they fail to exercise their "responsibility to exercise reasonable care to control his or her child in order to prevent harm to others."

Or you can be liable because your child is under the age of criminal responsibility (This age varies for state crimes; 33 states have no set minimum age. For federal crimes, the minimum age of criminal responsibility is 11). If your child is below that age and breaks the law, you could be put on trial on their behalf.

It's never a good idea to ignore potentially illegal behavior.

WHAT IS ILLEGAL?

The following things are age restricted in most countries and illegal in others:

- Regular pornography
- Adult dating services
- Age-restricted movies, television, and video games
- Online gambling

The following things are illegal for everyone in most countries:

- Child pornography
- Violent or nonconsensual pornography
- Illegal drugs
- Restricted drugs purchased without a prescription
- Illegally downloaded movies, TV shows, and games
- Hacking tools

STAYING OUT OF TROUBLE

One simple way to stay out of trouble involves breaking down the Internet into tiers of safety. These are:

Tier 1—Free access

This consists of the free sites hosted by the major Internet companies or broadcasters. They are generally policed by administrators who will deal with any problematic users or content as soon as they are made aware of them. Kids' areas are clearly allocated, and age-appropriate warnings or blocks are placed on adult content (although these are often easy to get through). Sites include Google, YouTube, Facebook, Instagram, Wikipedia, Reddit, Twitch, CNN, and the BBC.

Tier 2—Access permitted with parental supervision

These are sites that require credit or debit card payment to access their services, such as online shopping sites or subscription-based streaming services. This means your child will be assumed to be over 18 if they are using the site without parental controls being set, and it can give them the ability to spend money on your account. Sites include Amazon, Netflix, Hulu, and ESPN.

Tier 3—Restricted

The final tier is the part of the Internet that requires Tor to access. These sites sell products like illegal drugs, weapons, hacking tools, and even stolen identities.

I would strongly recommend that you make sure your child never accesses sites in tier 3, and that if they have access to tier 2, it is with your supervision and using the correct permissions (i.e., don't allow your child to log in to Netflix at home or on their device using their friend's account; they should access it through an account that you can control). You should also make sure your child doesn't know the password to these sites so that you maintain control over your bank cards and can set parental controls. See pp.228–229 for guidance on risks for children at different ages.

THERE'S ILLEGAL CONTENT ON MY CHILD'S DEVICE—WHAT DO I DO?

This is obviously the nightmare all parents fear. However, there are considerations to think about before you get angry. Don't assume that your child downloaded the material deliberately or that it's part of a wider pattern. It's possible that:

- Somebody else sent it to them/downloaded it onto their device.
- They looked at it only out of curiosity.
- Someone else made them download it.

Refer to the chapter "Talking to Your Kids" when discussing the content you have found with your child. In most cases, your order of action should be:

1. **Find and delete all the material.** Search all their devices and any USB drives to find out how much of the material there is. The more illegal material there is and the harder things are to find, the more likely the behavior is habitual rather than a one-off incident. If you're not going to refer the issue to a third party, delete all the material.

2. **Educate your child.** Explain to them that what they have is illegal, why it is inappropriate, and the potential risks of them having it—prosecution or parental prosecution.

3. **Identify the source.** Find out where this material came from. This will help you evaluate whether the matter needs to be referred to a counselor or even the police.

4. **Refer to a third party.** If you can't talk reasonably to your child, they don't seem to be understanding the seriousness of the situation, or they are viewing illegal material habitually or addictively, refer your child to counseling. If your child is involved in illegal activity, you need to speak to some form of law enforcement agency. Not doing so is an offense and may make you an accessory to the crime. However, there is a world of difference between a couple of accidental downloads and serious criminal behavior. If you suspect that an online predator might be targeting your child, go to the police.

CHILD PORNOGRAPHY

This is the most serious of all the illegal material listed on this page. If your child has these images on their computer, it may be a sign that they are being targeted by an abuser.

1. Evaluate the situation. Start by giving your child the benefit of the doubt. If the images are of a girlfriend or boyfriend, your child might not realize the content is illegal. If so, delete the images and make sure your child understands why.

2. Dig deeper. If the images aren't of a boyfriend or girlfriend, tread very carefully. Find out if your child knows the person in the pictures and where the images came from.

3. If you suspect an adult or older child is involved, you must contact the police. The people who abuse children will continue to do so until caught. Consider getting a counselor to talk to your child as they may be distressed by the images.

GATHERING EVIDENCE

WHAT YOU NEED AND HOW TO GET IT

If you need to involve a third party, such as a teacher, a website administrator, or the police, the more evidence of the problem or crime you have, the better. It is particularly important when it comes to dangerous behavior, such as online grooming. Without evidence, law enforcement agencies can't investigate or apprehend the culprit(s) and prevent them from harming anyone else. Don't delete anything; it could be the proof you need to solve the situation.

WHAT YOU NEED TO PROVE

You want to be able to prove as many of the following things:

- **Who was involved?** Just your child and the perpetrator, or others, too?
- **What happened?** Was it something the perpetrator said or did? How can you prove it is a serious issue?
- **Where?** Was it in a chat room, an app, a social media page, by email? Make sure you log every platform the perpetrator used.
- **When?** Time, date, and location. Was it every time your child logged on? Is this the same time each day?

HOW TO PROVE IT

Use screenshots or video recordings of the following things to prove what happened. Make sure to include the time and date each item was sent or posted, the usernames of those involved, and the web address of the site or app.

- Chat messages
- Texts
- Emails
- Message content
- Images, videos, GIFs, or memes received
- Screenshots of or links to the website or other pages

SECURING THE EVIDENCE

It's important to make sure you don't lose any of the evidence you have gathered.

1. Take the device away from your child. You may wish to do this if the content on the device might distress them or you fear that they might damage the evidence saved on it.

2. Keep the evidence on the original device. This may be crucial if the police need to use the device itself as evidence.

3. Save a copy. Ensure that there is a copy of the evidence on a USB memory stick or external hard drive in case the device is lost or damaged.

TAKING SCREENSHOTS

Instructions for taking screenshots on different devices can be seen below.

WINDOWS COMPUTER

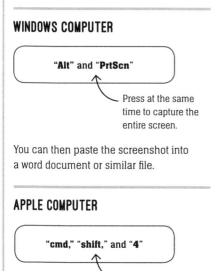

"Alt" and "PrtScn"

Press at the same time to capture the entire screen.

You can then paste the screenshot into a word document or similar file.

APPLE COMPUTER

"cmd," "shift," and "4"

Press at the same time to capture a section of the screen.

You can then click and drag the cursor to create a box over the area you want to capture or press the space bar and click on a window to capture an entire window. The screenshot appears on your desktop.

CELL PHONES AND TABLETS

Taking screenshots on these devices varies from device to device, so look up instructions for your child's device on the manufacturer's website.

TAKING SCREEN RECORDINGS

It may be difficult to screenshot everything that happens in a chat room because messages can disappear under new messages quickly. If this is the case, your child may want to take a screen recording (a video of what is happening on their screen) so they capture everything. Remember, they can always take a video of their computer screen using their cell phone's camera.

WINDOWS COMPUTER

"Windows" and "G"

Press at the same time to open the "**Game bar**"

Press the red button on the bar to start the recording. A smaller bar with a timer will then appear. To stop the recording, click on the red square next to the timer. You can view the recording in the Xbox app (found in the apps list). When the Xbox app is open, click on the Game DVR icon on the left of the window. This will bring up your screen recordings.

APPLE COMPUTER

Use QuickTime player to take a screen recording.

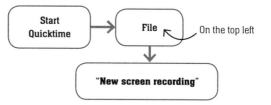

Start Quicktime → **File** — On the top left

↓

"New screen recording"

This will take a video of everything that happens on-screen. To stop recording, right-click on the QuickTime icon at the bottom of the screen and select "Stop recording."

CELL PHONES AND TABLETS

Taking screenshots and screen recordings on these devices varies from device to device, so look up instructions for your device on the manufacturer's website.

AGES AND STAGES When should you let your child do what?*

	AGES 3–5	AGES 6–9
WHAT'S THEIR EXPOSURE? How your child is likely to engage with the Internet and what sort of access you should give them	• Adult-guided activities (e.g., video calling family members) • Apps on parents' phones (e.g., games, YouTube) • Cameras and video cameras on parents' phones • Information shared about young children by their parents online	• Some have a personal device and are beginning to communicate independently • Entertainment, movies, TV, video (e.g., YouTube, Netflix) • Games and closed platforms • Internet access through game consoles and handheld devices
WHAT ARE THE RISKS? What type of issues might arise from your child browsing the Internet and using technology, and what you should look out for	• Forming lasting digital habits • Unaware of the risk of information sharing and appliances (e.g., baby monitors, household appliances) • Potential for exposure to adult content • Become aware of feedback from others on social media	• Unaware of tracking/privacy issues so open with personal information • Exposure to adult content • Don't understand they are receiving targeted ads • Forming lasting digital habits • Managing use can be difficult due to children's limited ability to self-regulate; this can cause family tension
WHAT CAN YOU DO? How you can help your child stay safe and get the most from the Internet and their devices	• Make sure all use of technology at this age is guided by adults • Make screen time a sociable time, involving older siblings and parents together	• Talk about the risks and benefits the Internet provides, checking your child's understanding • Ensure screen time takes up a minority of free time so your child develops social, emotional, and cognitive skills away from devices • Check devices have appropriate parental and security settings

*The ages given here are just a guide; exposure and risks may occur earlier or later for your child

AGES 10-12	AGES 13-15	AGES 16-18

- Children often get their first phone during transition to secondary school

- Likely to watch TV and movies, shop and game online, and use the Internet for homework research

- Open communication across a range of sites, including games and social media

	• Schoolwork has a digital component	
	• May access music, movies, and software. on illegal and unregulated sites	
	• Using the Internet to find groups they can identify with and join	

- Data profiling (targeted suggestions and ads)

- Cyberbullying, social isolation

	• Choosing to access adult content	
• Sharing personal information with little privacy, including photos	• May develop patterns of addictive use (e.g., gaming and shopping)	
	• Start to develop social anxiety and body image issues	• Risk of identity fraud grows with increase in online activities, such as shopping online
• Lack of critical analysis of information such as "fake news" and gossip on social media	• Unaware of impact of digital footprint—unlikely to think about consequences before acting	
	• Family tensions about extended digital activity	

• Use age-appropriate settings and safety features	• Acknowledge that this is an age of growing autonomy, so advice about digital use should be communicated with openness using noncontrolling language	• Continue to provide support and guidance as your child may not be able to view the world as an adult does until mid-20s
• Talk to your child about online experiences; this is vital for setting up a noncritical dialogue about the digital world		• Encourage older siblings to guide their younger family members' digital experiences
• Help them understand age restrictions on sites and apps	• Encourage achievements, relationships, and self-esteem in nondigital environments	

GLOSSARY

A

ad blocker software that prevents advertisements, such as pop-ups, from appearing on your screen

administrator (also "admin") for websites who monitor the behavior of the website and the user experience

ana a term used by pro-anorexia websites for the eating disorder anorexia

Alexa a "virtual assistant" created by Amazon that responds to voice commands and questions

Android a mobile operating system used on all tablets and smartphones, except Apple devices; see also *operating system*

anonymity program software, such as VPN and Tor, that enables users to browse the Internet without revealing their device or location

app a cell phone or computer program (or "application") that is downloaded onto a cell phone, tablet, or computer

B

bloatware software that is preinstalled by the manufacturer and may be of little or no use to the user

blog/blogger a website, often personal, that is updated regularly and usually written in conversational style; a vlog is a video form of a blog

bluejacking (also "bluehacking") when a stranger connects to a device via Bluetooth, allowing them to send unsolicited messages or to take control of the device

Bluetooth technology that allows you to connect devices wirelessly within a short range

bot software that can perform automated tasks, such as "liking" social media posts

C

catfishing when a person entraps someone else by pretending to be someone they're not

chat room a website, or "virtual venue," where a group of users can communicate in real time, usually about a specific topic

cloud shorthand for "cloud computing," the cloud refers to software or services that run on the Internet

cookies data about your online activity, which is collected when you visit websites

cyberbullying bullying that takes place online, often via nasty messages, comments, or images on social media

cybercrime criminal activity either using or directed at technology, such as hacking

cyberstalking when victims are persistently monitored and often followed across multiple digital or online platforms, such as email, chat rooms, or social media

D

data analytics company organizations that examine personal data harvested from users' online activity to identify and analyze patterns and behavior; companies use this information to improve their business and target consumers

data backup a copy of the data on a particular device stored externally—this may be on the cloud or on a hard drive

dark web the parts of the Internet that require anonymity programs to access, often used for illegal activity

domain an online identification system, or address, needed to access websites and emails

E

encryption when data is encoded and protected for security purposes so it can't be read by "unauthorized" persons

F

factory reset wipes all data, apps, and settings from a device, returning it to the state in which it left the manufacturer

"fake friend" when someone sends out online friend requests via a false online profile; see also *catfishing*

filters (images) software that uses techniques to modify or enhance features in an image

filters (Internet) software installed on devices that blocks certain websites, or categories of website; filters are often used to protect younger users from inappropriate online content

Find My Device a program that allows device owners to use any web browser to locate, lock, or erase data from their device

Find My Friends an app that allows users to reveal their device's (i.e., their) location to selected friends

firewall a security system implemented by either software or hardware that blocks unauthorized access to a private device

G

GIF usually a short animation, without sound, played on a loop

grooming the manipulative process used to maliciously control a child, often with the aim of sexual abuse

H

hacker (hack) someone who breaks into a device, account, network, or service without the owner's permission

hard drive a physical disk on which computer data is stored

hashtag the symbol "#" used at the beginning of a word on social media; this makes the term searchable so you can identify all posts on the same theme

hotspot a device that emits a Wi-Fi network allowing devices to connect to the Internet; see also *tethering*

human hacking the process of manipulating a person without their awareness; see also *grooming*

I

IP address the identification number associated with a device or Internet connection point

instant messaging any service that instantly transfers text between one or more users, e.g., text or messaging apps

Internet of Things (IoT) the population of physical devices that are able to connect to the Internet to perform a function (e.g., smart TVs or speakers, virtual assistants, and Wi-Fi-based home technology)

J

jailbreak when the operating software on a smartphone or tablet is altered to remove the manufacturer's restrictions; this allows users to install spyware and illegally downloaded apps

L

live game-streaming sites these sites allow users to broadcast a live video of computer games as they are playing them

M

malware "malicious software," such as viruses or spyware, that are designed to damage, disrupt, or access a device

mia a term used by pro-bulimia websites for bulimia

meme an image, video, or message shared online, usually with a humorous content

mod (game) a download that alters the appearance or function of a specific video game

moderator (also "mod") manages and monitors guests and users in chat rooms and "forums"; see also *administrator*

O

operating system (OS) the base software on a device that runs all the device's most basic functions (e.g., allowing the user to select and open apps); see also *Android*

online forum a set of public pages where users can exchange comments (often on a theme established by the initiator)

P

pagejacking a fake site that is imitating a legitimate site for an Internet service, shop, or company, often to trick users into revealing their personal data or account details; see also *phishing*

phishing sending fake emails appearing to be from a legitimate service to trick the recipient into visiting a fake site or downloading malicious software

pop-ups Internet browser windows that open without the user's permission, often containing advertisements of an explicit nature

private browsing a setting that prevents the browser from saving Internet history (the list of sites visited by the user) or usernames and passwords for sites visited

R

ransomware malicious software that locks a computer's content and demands payment to unlock it

S

scareware a type of fake ransomware

sextortion when someone is blackmailed about an explicit message or image they've sent or that has been hacked

socially engineer gaining someone's trust online to obtain personal information and then exploit them; see also *grooming*

social influencers people who have a significant online following that they can use to influence others

solid state drive (SSD) a type of external storage device that is used to back up data and has no moving parts

smart tech physical devices, such as appliances and toys, that can be controlled remotely via the Internet; see also *Internet of Things (IoT)*

spyware software that is surreptitiously installed on a person's device to obtain personal data and spy on their online activity

T

tethering the sharing of one device's Internet connection with other connected devices; see also *hotspot*

tracking following someone's activity online; see also *cookies*

troll someone who repeatedly makes irrelevant, and often malicious, comments on other people's social media posts.

two-factor authentication (2FA) a system that requires two passwords to be entered for the account to be accessed or a purchase verified; one is the standard account password, and the other is a randomly generated code sent to an elected email address or phone number each time someone tries to log in

V

viral a message, image, or video that is shared rapidly online

virtual private network (VPN) a private network software that encrypts users' device IP allowing them to connect to websites and use public networks securely; see also *IP address*

W

webcam a camera that captures and transmits video content

Z

"zombie" accounts unused and inactive social media and bank accounts

RESOURCES

The Carnegie Cyber Academy
www.carnegiecyberacademy.com

Child Online Protection
www.itu.int/en/cop

Child Protective Services
www.dshs.wa.gov/ca/parent-resources/
child-protective-services

Child Welfare Information Gateway
www.childwelfare.gov

Childnet International
www.childnet.com

Common Sense Media: Parent Concerns
www.commonsensemedia.org/
parent-concerns

Concerned Parents Toolbox
www.backgroundchecks.org/the-
concerned-parents-toolbox-120-tools-
and-tricks-to-protect-your-kids.html

ConnectSafely
www.connectsafely.org

Crime Stoppers USA
www.crimestoppersusa.org

CyberTipline
www.missingkids.com/gethelpnow/
cybertipline

Family Safe Computers
www.familysafecomputers.org

FBI Resources: Parents
www.fbi.gov/resources/parents

FTC Consumer Information: Protecting Kids Online
www.consumer.ftc.gov/topics/
protecting-kids-online

Internet Safety 101
www.internetsafety101.org

Kids Against Bullying
www.pacerkidsagainstbullying.org

Microsoft Digital Skills: Online Safety Resources
www.microsoft.com/en-us/digital-skills/
online-safety-resources

Save the Children
www.savethechildren.org/us/what-we-
do/us-programs/child-protection

Stop. Think. Connect.
www.dhs.gov/stopthinkconnect

Stopbullying.gov
www.stopbullying.gov

WebWiseKids
www.webwisekids.org

BIBLIOGRAPHY

Talking to Your Kids p.13 "Parents, Teens and Digital Monitoring," M. Anderson, Jan 7, 2016, Pew Research Center, pewinternet.org; p.14 "Teenagers 'more confident talking to each other via smartphones than face-to-face' – study," L. Peacock & R. Sanghani, Apr 29, 2014, telegraph.co.uk. **Creating a Healthy Tech Environment** p.24 "Social media and children's mental health: A review of the evidence," E. Frith, June 30, 2017, Education Policy Institute, epi.org.uk; p.25 "Americans check their phones 80 times a day: Study," SWNS, Nov 8, 2017, nypost.com; "Millennials and technology at home," Qualtrics and Accel, 2017, in 'The Surprising Reason Millennials Check Their Phones 150 Times a Day," J. Brandon, Apr 17, 2017, inc.com; p.26 "Millennials and technology at home," Qualtrics and Accel. **Chatting Online** p.32 "Shock stats: Your 13-year-old is SEXTING (and your 12-year-old is talking to strangers)," F. Thistlewaite, Aug 10, 2015, express.co.uk; p.33 "Online overtakes TV as kids' top pastime," Ofcom, Nov 16, 2016, ofcom.org.uk; p.34 "Internet Statistics," Guardchild, Feb 12, 2016, Guardchild.com; "Children using social networks underage 'exposes them to danger,'" R. Williams, Feb 6, 2016, telegraph.co.uk; p.37 "Internet Statistics," Guardchild, Feb 12, 2016, guardchild.com; p.38; p.42 "Online gaming among children in the United Kingdom," The Statistics Portal, Mar 1, 2018; p.44 "Stats About Online Predators and Precautions Parents Should Take," V. Kemp, Mar 12, 2012, patch.com. **Social Media** p.49 "Children and parents: Media use and attitudes report," Ofcom, Nov 29, 2017, ofcom. org.uk; p.50 "Sean Parker unloads on Facebook: S. Parker interviewed in 'God only knows what it's doing to our children's brains,'" M. Allen, Nov 9, 2017, axios.com; p.52 "The Power of 'Like,'" L. D. Rosen PhD, Jul 15, 2012, psychologytoday.com; p.57 "Online overtakes TV as kids' top pastime," Ofcom, Nov 16, 2016, ofcom.org.uk; p.58 "Clinical report—The impact of social media on children, adolescents, and families," G. Schurgin O'Keeffe, K. Clarke-Pearson & Council on Communications and Media, Mar 28, 2011, Pediatrics; p.61 "Internet trends 2014 – Code Conference," M. Meeker, May 28, 2014, kpcb.com. **Cyberbullying and Trolls** p.68 "Children and parents: Media use and attitudes report," Ofcom, Nov 29, 2017, ofcom.org.uk; p.69 "Internet trolling: Quarter of teenagers suffered online abuse last year," A. Gani, Feb 9, 2016, guardian.com; p.70 ibid.; p.72 "Children and parents: Media use and attitudes report," Ofcom, Nov 29, 2017, ofcom.org.uk; p.74 "Net Children Go Mobile: The UK Report," S. Livingston et al., Jul 2014, London School of Economics and Political Science; p.75 "The Annual Bullying Survey 2013: UK Bullying Statistics," Ditch the Label, Feb 3, 2013, ditchthelabel.org; p.77 "Facebook admits up to 270m users are fake and duplicate accounts," J. Titcomb, Nov 2, 2017; p.78 ibid.; p.80 "The Annual Bullying Survey 2017: UK Bullying Statistics," Ditch the Label, Jul 2017, ditchthelabel.org. **Cyberstalking and Tracking** p.84 "The Internet Problem We Don't Talk Enough About," M.Buxton, Mar 15, 2017, refinery29.com; p.89 "Online Harassment, Digital Abuse, and Cyberstalking in America," A. Lenhart et al., Nov 21, 2016, datasociety. net. **Grooming** p.98 "A study of disclosures of childhood abuse," NSPCC, Jul 1, 2013, nspcc.org; p.99 "Online Grooming Survey 2016," G. Kalkan & C.Fox, Dec 2016, barnardos.org.uk; p.100 "Facebook admits

up to 270m users are fake and duplicate accounts," Abcom IT solutions, Oct 19, 2013, abcom.co.uk; "Online Human-Bot Interactions: Detection, Estimation, and Characterization," O. Varrol et al., Mar 27, 2017, University of Southern Carolina; p.103 "Online Grooming Survey 2016," G. Kalkan & C. Fox, Dec 2016, barnardos.org.uk; p.112 "Teenage Sexting Statistics," Guardchild, Feb 12, 2016, guardchild. com; p.113 ibid.; p.114 ibid.; p.116 "Teenage Sexting Statistics," PCSNDreams: Internet predator protection, Feb 1, 2016, pcsndreams. com; p.118 "Boy, five, is 'youngest person in Britain' investigated by police for sexting," Telegraph, Jul 11, 2017, telegraph.co.uk; p.120; "11 Facts about Sexting," DoSomething, Apr 14, 2014, doSomething.org. **Pornography and Violent Content** p.124 "Internet Crime and Abuse Statistics," Guardchild: protecting children in the digital age, Feb 12, 2016, guardchild.com; p.126 "The impact of online pornography on the values, attitudes, beliefs and behaviours of children," E.Martellozo et al., May 2016, NSPCC; p.130 "Pornography desensitising young people," K. Sellgreen, June 15, 2016, BBC.co.uk. **Coercion, Extortion, and Blackmail** p.136 "Sextortion: Cybersecurity, teenagers, and remote sexual assault," B. Wittes et al., May 11, 2016, brookings.edu; p.140 "Sextortion," S. Hinduja, June 28, 2016, cyberbullying.org; p.141 "Alarm over steep rise in number of sextortion cases in UK," S. Marsh, Sep 3, 2017, guardian.com; p.142 "4 Ways Artificial Intelligence Benefits Web Hosting," WebHosting, Feb 8, 2018, webhosting.uk. **Online Shopping** p.150 "Counterfeit Goods Are a $460 Billion Industry, and Most Are Bought and Sold Online," R.Klare, Feb 14, 2017, adweek.com; p.151 "Identity fraud soars to new levels," S.Samee, Aug 23, 2017, cifas.org.uk; p.152 "Identity Fraud Hit 15.4 Million U.S. Victims in 2016: Report," I. Arghire, Feb 2, 2017, securityweek.com; p.155 "Are fake online reviews killing consumer confidence?" T. Weinberg, Oct 21, 2016, marketingland.com; p.159 "1 in 4 Wi-Fi Hotspots Just Waiting to Be Hacked" Kaspersky Lab, Nov 24, 2016, kaspersky.com; p.160 "The app economy could double to $101 billion by 2020," D. Takahashi, Feb 10, 2016, venturebeat.com; p.161 "4 eye-opening facts about phishing," M. Samarati, Dec 14, 2016, itgovernance.co.uk. **Cosmetics, Drugs, and Legal Highs** p.167 "Operations," Interpol: Operation Pangea, June 9, 2015, interpol.int; p.170 "Health fears over boys as young as 13 using steroids," S. Morris, Jan 22, 2018, guardian.com; p.172 "Muscle-enhancing Behaviors Among Adolescent Girls and Boys," M. Eisenberg et al., Nov 1, 2012, pediatrics.aappublications.org; p.173 "CCBYNC Evaluation of symptom checkers for self diagnosis and triage: Audit study," H. Semigran et al., June 15, 2015, thebmj.com; p.175 "Cybermedicine: The Benefits and Risks of Purchasing Drugs Over The Internet," D. Mills, June 1, 2000, Journal of Technology Law & Policy (vol.5). **Smart Tech and Toys** p.183 "IoT to have 75 billion 'connected' devices by 2025," Global Sources, May 5, 2016, globalsources.com; p.187 "13 stunning stats on the Internet of Things," K. Claveria, Apr 28, 2017, visioncritical.com; p.188 "Dozens of Canon security cameras hacked in Japan," A. Presse, May 7, 2018, nationmultimedia.com. **Your Child's Digital Footprint** p.198 "Profiling employees online: Shifting public–private boundaries in organisational life," P. McDonald et al., Aug 15, 2016, onlinelibrary.wiley.com.

INDEX

ABOUT WILL GEDDES

With more than 25 years' experience, Will Geddes is recognized as a leading specialist security advisor. He has worked for royal families, former heads of state, and Hollywood celebrities, as well as FTSE 100 and Fortune 500 companies. Beginning his professional career in human threat management (HTM), Will has operated around the world, including in hostile and high-risk environments, such as Iraq, Afghanistan, and Syria, and has been strategically and tactically involved in cyber security, counterterrorism, extortion management, emergency extractions, intelligence gathering, and investigations. He is also a regular keynote speaker and an advisor to The International Press and Media Group.

ABOUT NADIA & KAYE

Best friends and television presenters Nadia Sawalha and Kaye Adams are well known for being panelists on the long-running ITV daytime chat show *Loose Women*.

Nadia originally rose to fame as an actress, appearing as Annie Palmer in the BBC's *EastEnders* and went on to win *Celebrity MasterChef* in 2007.

Kaye, meanwhile, is a highly respected journalist, having made her name reporting current affairs for ITV and STV and with a daily current affairs program on BBC Scotland, *The Kaye Adams Programme*.

Together, the pair host their own YouTube channel, *Nadia & Kaye*, and Facebook page, where they vlog about a range of subjects. At the time of writing, their YouTube channel has just under 20,000 subscribers, and their "Parent Alert!" video, which was the starting point for this book, has been viewed more than 28 million times on Facebook.

ACKNOWLEDGMENTS

THE AUTHORS WOULD LIKE TO THANK:

Will: I'd like to thank Nadia and Kaye, who have been great allies and collaborators, with their no-nonsense advice and perspective; my agent, Nicola, for her support, drive, and belief in proposing me to the amazing team at DK—MC, Stephanie, Toby, Lisa, and Kathryn. I'd also like to thank the many "true" cyber experts I've worked with and learned from over the years, including Tom G., James T., Prof Neil B., Mark S., Mark W.–T. and those many other friends working tirelessly in front of and behind the scenes on child protection.

Nadia: Thank you to my darling daughter Maddie for bringing Snap Map to our attention—YOU made this book a possibility! My clever, kind, beautiful girl. Thank you to Will Geddes—you are a scholar and a gentleman and our very own James Bond! You have grafted like a nutter! Thank you to Nicola Ibison, a damn fine agent with a razor-sharp brain and a talent for books! Thank you to the brilliant team at DK—the best publishers in the world! I love being part of the family!

Kaye: I don't know whether to thank Will Geddes or curse him! To say he has opened my eyes to some of the pitfalls of the digital world is an understatement. However, as they say, forewarned is forearmed so, on reflection, a very sincere "Thank you, Will." Many thanks also to our agent, Nicola, who pushed us into following up on the incredible response to our Snap Map video with this book, and to the incredible team at DK— hardworking, creative, smart, and makers of very fine cake.

DK WOULD LIKE TO THANK:

Angharad Rudkin, PsyD, child clinical psychologist and program tutor at the University of Southampton, for writing the "Ages and Stages" section and for casting her professional eye over the entirety of the book. Carrie Marshall for her writing and knowledge; Vicky Read, Steven Marsden, Philippa Nash, and Hannah Moore for their artwork; Poppy Blakiston-Houston for editorial assistance; Vicky Read and Philippa Nash for design assistance; Anna Cheifetz for proofreading; and Marie Lorimer for the index.

Senior editors Claire Cross, Lisa Dyer, Kathryn Meeker
US editor Jennette ElNaggar
US consultant Michael Miller
Senior art editors Glenda Fisher, Hannah Moore
Editors Alice Horne, Toby Mann
Jacket designer Maxine Pedliham
Jackets co-ordinator Lucy Philpott
Producer, pre-production Robert Dunn
Senior producer Stephanie McConnell
Creative technical support Sonia Charbonnier
Managing editor Stephanie Farrow
Managing art editor Christine Keilty
Art director Maxine Pedliham
Publishing director Mary-Clare Jerram

Contributing writer Carrie Marshall
Photographer Noel Murphy

First American Edition, 2018
Published in the United States by DK Publishing
345 Hudson Street, New York, New York 10014

Copyright © 2018 Dorling Kindersley Limited
DK, a Division of Penguin Random House LLC
Text © 2018 Nadia Sawalha, Kaye Adams, and William Geddes
18 19 20 21 22 10 9 8 7 6 5 4 3 2 1
001–311050–Jul/2018

A catalog record for this book is available from the Library of Congress.
ISBN: 978-1-4654-7725-5
Printed and bound in Canada

A WORLD OF IDEAS:
SEE ALL THERE IS TO KNOW

www.dk.com